PREGNANCY GUIDE FOR MEN

HOW TO BE THE BEST SUPPORTIVE PARTNER AND FATHER, FROM CONCEPTION TO BIRTH AND BEYOND. PLUS 10 LIFE HACKS FOR NEW DADS

NEW DAD SUPPORT

CONTENTS

Bonuses — vi
Introduction — ix

1. BECOMING A DAD — 1
   Preparing to Get Pregnant — 2
   Preparing Yourself Mentally — 4
   Preparing Your Relationship — 6

2. YOU'RE PREGNANT! — 11
   Revealing the Pregnancy — 12
   The Fun Stuff — 14

3. BIRTHING AND BUILDING A BIRTH PLAN — 23
   Where to Deliver — 24
   Methods of Birthing — 27
   Birth Plans — 31

4. PREPARING FOR THE WORST — 35
   Miscarriages and Stillbirth — 36
   Ectopic Pregnancy — 37
   Infertility — 38
   Possible Pregnancy Complications — 41
   Screenings and Tests — 49

5. FIRST TRIMESTER — 57
   Week 1 & 2 — 58
   Week 3 — 59
   Week 4 — 60
   Week 5 — 62
   Week 6 — 63
   Week 7 — 66
   Week 8 — 67
   Week 9 — 69
   Week 10 — 70

Week 11	73
Week 12	75
6. SECOND TRIMESTER	**77**
Week 13	78
Week 14	80
Week 15	83
Week 16	87
Week 17	89
Week 18	91
Week 19	93
Week 20	95
Week 21	97
Week 22	98
Week 23	99
Week 24	100
Week 25	102
Week 26	104
7. THIRD TRIMESTER	**107**
Week 27	108
Week 28	110
Week 29	111
Week 30	112
Week 31	114
Week 32	115
Weeks 33 - 40+	116
8. GETTING READY FOR BIRTH	**119**
Essentials for Baby's Arrival	120
Hospital Go-Bag Essentials	127
Signs of Labor	131
The Birth	133
9. THE FOURTH TRIMESTER	**137**
Finding Your Routine	138
Supporting Mom's Recovery	141
Going Back to Work	143

10. NEW DAD HACKS	147
Pregnancy Hacks	148
Newborn Hacks	148
Afterword	151
Review	154
Bonuses	155
References	157
About the Author	161

Free Bonuses

Free Bonus #1   Baby Financial Planning

In this book, you will learn all about the financial considerations of having a baby.

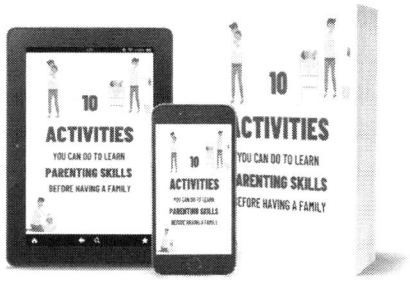

Free Bonus #2   10 Activities to Learn Parenting Skills

In this book, you will get tips on how to build parenting skills even before the baby is born.

Free Bonus #3 Authentic Connections

In this book, you will learn new skills to help you nurture your connection with your partner and bring it to a whole new level.

To get bonuses, scan this QR code with your cell phone

© Copyright 2022 by TFIG LLC - All rights reserved.

The content contained within this book may not be reproduced, duplicated or transmitted without direct written permission from the author or the publisher.

Under no circumstances will any blame or legal responsibility be held against the publisher, or author, for any damages, reparation, or monetary loss due to the information contained within this book, either directly or indirectly.

Legal Notice:

This book is copyright protected. It is only for personal use. You cannot amend, distribute, sell, use, quote or paraphrase any part, or the content within this book, without the consent of the author or publisher.

Disclaimer Notice:

Please note the information contained within this document is for educational and entertainment purposes only. All effort has been executed to present accurate, up to date, reliable, complete information. No warranties of any kind are declared or implied. Readers acknowledge that the author is not engaged in the rendering of legal, financial, medical or professional advice. The content within this book has been derived from various sources. Please consult a licensed professional before attempting any techniques outlined in this book.

By reading this document, the reader agrees that under no circumstances is the author responsible for any losses, direct or indirect, that are incurred as a result of the use of the information contained within this document, including, but not limited to, errors, omissions, or inaccuracies.

ISBN: Print 978-1-95854-103-6

INTRODUCTION

> "Making the decision to have a child is momentous. It is to decide forever to have your heart go walking around outside your body." – Elizabeth Stone

So, it's officially time. You and your partner have decided to pursue growing your family. First, congratulations on taking the next incredible step on your journey! Becoming a parent is a monumental and life-changing step in anyone's life. Making the choice to become parents takes your relationship to the next level, and though we may know people who are parents—we may have watched all kinds of media about having a child, or read articles and books—nothing can truly prepare us for the wonder that is pregnancy, childbirth, and parenthood until we're in the thick of it.

Today, the responsibilities of each parent is shifting; more families rely on dual incomes than that of our grandparents, as well as some of our parents. The impact of pregnancy on the mind and body of those who bear children is better understood, and we can now better support our partners after they've brought our children into the world. We can better understand the pressures of parenting while working, making us better companions when our partner needs us the most.

In the following chapters, we cover the whole story of pregnancy from conception to birth and beyond. Everything from the possible complications and difficulties of conception and pregnancy, to how to be the best father and partner when the new baby is brought home.

 "A baby makes love stronger, the days shorter, the nights longer, savings smaller, and a home happier." —Unknown

CHAPTER 1
BECOMING A DAD

> "Fatherhood is the greatest thing that could ever happen. You can't explain it until it happens; it's like telling somebody what water feels like before they've ever swam in it." – Michael Bublé

IN THE MONTHS leading up to conception, there is work to be done to make sure that both you and your partner have balanced and healthy expectations of one another. When we first start planning to conceive, we can sometimes think that we just have to get romantic and intimate with our partner at the right time, and that's all there is to it. In a lot of cases, it can take time for the pregnancy to come about. Don't panic if you're not immediately pregnant because you did the deed exactly 14 days after the first day of your partner's period. There's plenty that can be done to help you and your partner get ready to conceive.

PREPARING TO GET PREGNANT

Physically, there is just as much that goes into Dad getting ready for the point of conception as there is for Mom. After all, you're looking to plant a high-quality seed here, and you want to be healthy if you're going to give yourself the best chance of conceiving. Choosing to conceive sometimes means starting months in advance so that you can hopefully have a healthy child without too much struggling to conceive. In order to give yourself the best chances of conception, the following list can help you increase your fertility:

- **Speak to your doctor.** Whether it's getting a physical or having your sperm count tested, speaking to your doctor can help you both get healthy, and possibly pinpoint any areas that may be working against you in conceiving a child with your partner. Your doctor will work with you to identify if there are any medications that you're on that may inhibit your ability to have a child, as well as look into any dietary or sleep changes that may need to be made. Depending on what you do for work, they may also advise you to stay away from certain types of chemicals, such as solvents and pesticides. Of course, adding in an exercise regimen if you don't already have one may be recommended.

- While you're there, get a better look at your medical history. Knowing if there are any serious diseases or genetic abnormalities that run in your family will help you know what to look for when you have your own child. If you know what you're up against, you can be better equipped for the possibilities regarding your child's health and well-being down the road.

- **Keep your boys cool.** If you're a briefs man, it may be time to trade them in for some boxers. The same goes for staying out of the sauna, the hot tub, or extra hot showers and baths. Heat can harm and kill the sperm cells that you're hoping to put to work, so making sure that your testicles are staying cool is a good way to help increase sperm count. There is still some debate over whether briefs are the biggest problem in terms of capturing and retaining heat, but especially if you're concerned about a low sperm count, getting some extra air flow in there can't hurt.

- **It's time to stop the party.** Alcohol, drugs, and cigarettes can all contribute to a lowered sperm count and even erectile dysfunction. If you're hoping to conceive, it's time to get rid of the intoxicants and focus on consuming healthier foods. Trade in the beer for a smoothie, and drop the smoking habit if you're hoping to boost the number of sperm you're working with.

- **Get the good food in you.** Having a balanced, nutritious diet can affect the health and motility of your swimmers.

We're talking lean proteins, fruits, veggies, and good carbs and fats, as well as a multivitamin. Potential Dads want a diet rich in zinc, folic acid, and vitamins A, C, and E to increase the health of their sperm and keep them mobile when it comes time to attempt conception.
- **Keep the laptop on the desk and the phone out of your front pocket.** Electromagnetic radiation is suspected to be one of the big culprits of negatively impacting healthy semen. Moving your phone away from your groin, as well as keeping your laptop up on your desk instead of in your lap can minimize this radiation. The same is true with the extra heat that is put out by the machinery that can kill sperm counts.

PREPARING YOURSELF MENTALLY

Some people can view the period of pregnancy as fairly hands-off for Dad; just make sure she gets her pregnancy cravings delivered when she wants them, and give her foot rubs when her feet swell, but after you've "planted the seed" your job is done. While yes, the brunt of the physical labor is on the new Mom, there are still things for you to prepare yourself for and educate yourself on. You're in on this team effort, even if the baby isn't firmly squared away in your abdomen to grow for 40 weeks.

Ultimately, your job is to support your partner through pregnancy and birth. Just by the act of having picked up this book, you're already starting one of the first things you can do; learn about what is going on in Mom's body while she is pregnant. Taking the time to learn about what she will go through while pregnant and delivering the baby can make you more compassionate, as well as better equipped with knowing how to handle anything the pregnancy and delivery hurls at you. Being aware of foods that might harm the baby, medications that can be safely used, and being ready to mentally and physically support your partner are crucial to having a safe and happy pregnancy.

If you're worried about feeling like you can't do anything to support your partner, do things like taking a massage class so you can ease any pain and discomfort that grows in her body over time. Look around the house and do things without being asked. After all, taking care of the home should be a team effort, and contrary to societal jokes about bossy women, most women really don't want to be the house manager. If you don't know how to cook—learn. If you don't usually take on laundry, floors, or other household chores—step up without your partner having to hound you or beg for your help. Especially when the baby arrives, doing all these things on top of raising the child, *and* trying to heal from a major medical event, can lead to worsening symptoms of postpartum depression and anxiety if your partner doesn't feel as though they have support. Women and mothers feeling that their partner isn't an equal contributor to the home are going to be more likely to leave. Even if she steps forward as a stay-at-home or work-from-home parent, remember that she is your partner, not your maid or slave. Raising children is no easy feat, and being a stay-at-home parent is more than just watching *Price is Right* and feeding the baby.

PREPARING YOUR RELATIONSHIP

It's so easy for us to think that nothing will change within the relationship just because you've become parents. This doesn't take into account the changes in mentality when your priorities shift to caring for your child, as well as the stress brought on by sleepless nights, the days of crying when the baby is teething or sick, or the struggles of disorders like postpartum depression, anxiety, or psychosis that Mom might face after giving birth.

Before you consider bringing a child into your life, really evaluate the health and stability of your relationship. Are you a stable and reliable partner to the person you hope will bear your child? Is she stable and ready to take on this major challenge with you? Are you two compassionate and loving towards each other, or do you tolerate each other because it's more comfortable to be with the person you can predict?

You should also consider why you and your partner are choosing to pursue having a child. Are you worried about an oncoming breakup, and think that it'll save your relationship? Or are you genuinely hoping and looking forward to raising a child with this person? Bringing a child into an unstable relationship won't save the relationship, or keep someone from leaving the relationship, so evaluate the reasons why you really want to have a child with this person.

When you've come to your conclusion, and if you've found it to be coming from a place of love, then look at how you can support your relationship's foundations going forward. If you have routines like doing date nights or movie nights, continue doing these things that are special to the two of you. Before the baby is conceived, make sure that your foundations with your partner are as stable as they can be. If you do have some concerns about moving forward, there is no shame in pursuing couples counseling if you feel your mutual understanding of each other could benefit the relationship. The most important thing about preparing your relationship before conceiving is making sure that the necessary pathways of communication are open and actively used.

Before conceiving, expectations for the pregnancy and after the baby's arrival should be spoken about and agreed upon. Get on the same page about changes in the routine, changes in scheduling, maternity and paternity leave, potential sitters, and other childcare and work schedules. These aren't things that you're going to want to fight about when you're in the thick of it. Even making sure that you're on the same page and a united front when it comes to things like discipline, religion, and schooling can go a long way in preventing major disagreements that could have been avoided. Take the time, and really paint out your vision for the future, and listen to your partner's vision of the future. It's perfectly normal for those visions to not perfectly align, but be prepared to compromise now, instead of later when you might learn just how different your views are compared to your partner.

Take some time to answer the questions below together.

1. Why do we want to start a family?

2. Is now the best time?

3. How much will it cost? Can we afford it?

4. Will we both continue to work after the birth? If so, what will we do for childcare?

5. How do we want to parent? How will we discipline?

6. What values or religious beliefs do we want to pass on?

7. How will we address issues in getting pregnant?

8. What does the future of our family look like? How many kids do we want? And how soon?

CHAPTER 2
YOU'RE PREGNANT!

> "Fathering is not something perfect men do, but something that perfects the man." – Frank Pittman

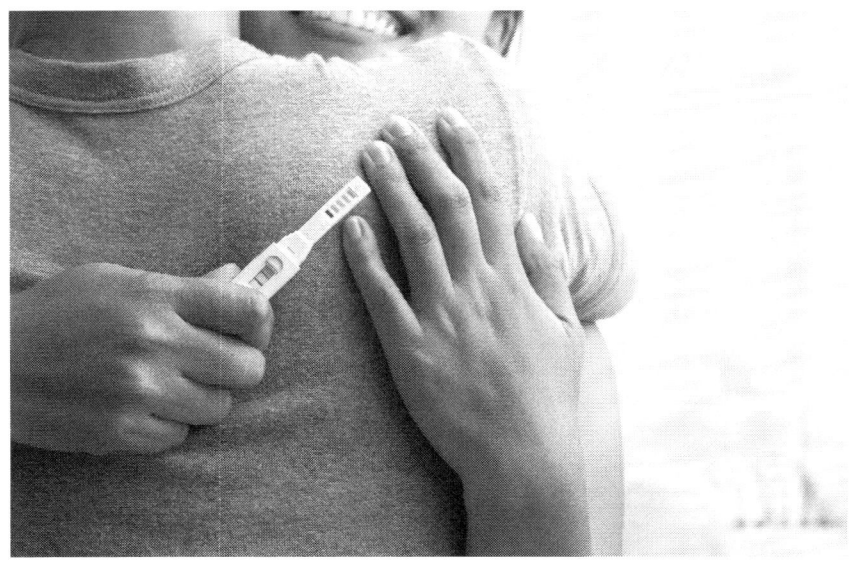

IT HAPPENED—YOU got through the obstacles, and now you've got that positive pregnancy test sitting on your counter. Before we get into the nitty-gritty of what's going on inside of Mom's uterus and how you can best help her, let's take a look at the fun stuff you get to do now that you're officially expecting.

REVEALING THE PREGNANCY

Pregnancy announcements vary per couple. Some people may wait until they're past the 12-week mark to negate the riskiest time period for miscarriage; others may be rushing out to tell everyone right away. There isn't a wrong way to go about announcing your pregnancy. When considering announcing the pregnancy, think about the following points so that you can best choose how and when to announce your newest arrival:

- Consider your timeline. If your partner has experienced a miscarriage before, give yourselves time to get past the riskiest period of time before announcing the pregnancy. At least this way, you can negate the painful reminders if a miscarriage does happen. Truly, there's no worse feeling after having just miscarried than seeing an acquaintance that asks about the pregnancy, just to be reminded of your loss and having to talk about it. If you want to be careful, take the time.
- Consider *who* you're telling. While we may be excited to tell everyone under the sun about the baby on the way, we also want to be able to break the news ourselves. Before you break out the big announcement, make sure that the people that you're telling early are people that

you trust—that aren't going to run their mouths and ruin the excitement of the announcement for you and your partner. If you know that someone on either side of the family is way too excited about becoming a grandparent, aunt, or uncle, consider waiting to tell them about the pregnancy until you're just about to announce it, so that they can't excitedly take the wind out of your sails.
- Who needs to be told before the main announcement? In the case of certain jobs that may be harmful to a pregnancy, Mom may need to tell her employer about the pregnancy sooner than later. This is particularly important if the job comes with a lot of heavy lifting, physical exertion, or working with potentially harmful chemicals.
- Aside from an employer, we all have a list of people who we know would be hurt if they weren't personally told about the pregnancy before the rest of the world finds out on social media, so talk to your partner about letting these people in on the secret and when.
- Plan the announcement itself. Nobody says that you have to have a major grand reveal, or that you have to go all the way out. Do what feels the most comfortable for both you and your partner, and what you feel is most representative of you as a couple and family. Some people use their pets as a way to introduce the pregnancy to the world, others like to do a photo set that goes up on social media. There are hundreds upon hundreds of ideas online if you're looking for inspiration.

THE FUN STUFF

The "fun stuff" is usually the keepsake items and family events that revolve around the pregnancy. These are events that you'll look back on and show your child. You'll want to record these special moments, where you can truly celebrate with those that matter the most to you. Some of these occasions will also be a chance to get a little bit of help from family and friends. This is so important when it comes to getting everything you need to help you care for your baby.

Weekly Progress Photos

You and your partner can really start this at any time. Some like to wait to start seeing the baby bump forming, and some like to take pictures right from the beginning so they can best see exactly when the baby bump started to form, and the changes that their body went through from start to finish. These progress photos are often cherished, and can make a fantastic collage, culminating with a picture of you holding the little one after you've gotten out of the hospital with Mom and baby.

Pregnancy Journal

Pregnancy journals are both a helpful resource and a lovely keepsake. This is where Mom can track all of the happenings in her pregnancy: different cravings, the variety of symptoms, the first kicks, absolutely anything she wants. Depending on her intent, it can become a keepsake item that is passed down to the child, or something that she keeps for herself. Bringing it to appointments with you can also help, so she can reference notes if there was a concerning symptom, to add in any sonogram pictures that are printed off, or to be able to easily reference questions she might have for the doctor, or any ideas that she might need confirmation on from her medical professional.

Bump Casting

Bump casting is using some form of plaster or otherwise skin-safe molding material to get a cast of the baby belly shortly before Mom gives birth. These can be turned into lovely art pieces to be decorated later with the baby's handprints, or made into a decorative sculpture to commemorate the pregnancy.

Baby Names

Choosing a baby name is just as fun as it can be intimidating. Are you going to choose a family name, or is the child going to get their own unique name? When choosing a baby name, there is one simple rule: it takes both parents saying "yes" for a name to be an option, but one "no" to take it off the table. If someone says no, the name needs to be dropped, and continue the search for a new name. If you're choosing not to find out the gender of the baby, it can help to have three name options: one feminine, one masculine, and one gender neutral. Some parents find that it helps to see the baby before choosing a name, so do what fits best for you.

Some people also choose to withhold the name until the baby arrives. This can be for a variety of reasons; some simply find it fun, and will refer to the baby as "Baby A" or something along those lines so that they can introduce the baby to the world with their real name. In other situations, if you know someone within the family is going to push for a family name that the two of you don't agree on—or especially if either of you have that one family member who insists that you name the baby after them for whatever reason—keeping the name secret keeps people from pushing opinions on the name that you're choosing for your child. It can also keep other people from attempting to ruin the name for you, depending on what your relationship is with your family.

Baby Showers/Diaper Parties

Depending on where you're from and any family traditions, some people may choose to throw their own baby shower, while others have family or friends throw the party on their behalf. There are a few variations on the traditional baby shower in more recent years. Traditionally, a baby shower is more for the women of the family and friend circle, and is primarily centered around Mom and baby. However, many have started to do them "Jack and Jill" style, centering around Mom and Dad. The baby shower is where you usually get lots of the baby essentials: clothes, toys, books, blankets—and depending on the financial situation of those participating, sometimes even strollers, high chairs, or whichever other gifts you may have listed on the baby registry to let people know what you need and what you'd like to have for the baby. Guests play games centered around the baby, like guessing how big the baby belly is, sometimes holding raffles regarding the baby's weight or when they'll make their appearance. Every area tends to hold their own baby shower traditions, but food, games, and lots of talk about the baby are typical for baby showers.

Diaper parties are often centered around Dad. While there are still some of the usual baby shower games present, diaper parties tend to be a little less "all about baby." Traditionally, the guests of the diaper party will bring one or two boxes of diapers each, enjoy a barbecue, and otherwise enjoy their own games. There may be betting on the baby's arrival, or other games involving the baby's weight or length when they are born, but just like the baby shower, the games and traditions tend to be reliant on the area that you are from.

Gender Reveals

Gender reveals can be fun… if done safely. The inventor of the gender reveal party, Jenna Karvunidis, has expressed her own horror and regret about the dangerous extremes that gender reveal parties have become. If you choose to have a gender reveal party, don't resort to explosives; as we've seen in the past, while we may enjoy having a dramatic announcement, do so with less fire and explosives that can result in wildfires and casualties. If you choose to have a gender reveal party with your loved ones, try popping balloons or cutting cakes with the color associated with your baby's gender hidden inside.

Baby Registry

The baby registry is a great way to let others help you, as well as a way to keep track of what you may still need to get. Parents tend to be hesitant of putting expensive items onto their registry, but don't fear the expensive items! Sometimes there are multiple people who want to pool funds to buy something larger, or someone may have the resources to buy the one you like. Other times, knowing that you still need something like a stroller may mean that other parents looking at your registry might already have the item in good shape to give to you. If the people looking to buy a gift for your child don't have the resources for the expensive items, letting them know what kinds of blankets, toys, and other supplies you may need lets them find something within their budget, and takes some pressure off of you and your partner. List anything you can think of, and refer to the registry regularly so that you know what you still need to get. Of course, this also helps your friends and family know what to get, instead of defaulting to a tiny onesie or another teddy bear.

Maternity Photos

These are the special mementos before and after the due date, where you can really capture the beauty of the pregnancy. Some people like to do this a few times over the course of the pregnancy, while some couples really like to wait until the bump is about as big as it's going to get. Doing a maternity shoot is a great way for an exhausted mother to feel beautiful, and for both Mom and Dad to really gain an appreciation for what her body is doing. Some maternity shoots are entirely focused on the mother, but lots of people also incorporate the father as well. After all, you certainly helped kickstart the pregnancy to begin with.

List 3 or more ideas of fun ways to announce the pregnancy.

PREGNANCY CHECKLIST

FIRST TRIMESTER

Calculate your baby's due date	Figure out your finances
Talk to your insurance company	Follow a healthy lifestyle
Choose a doctor/midwife	Take your prenatal vitamins
Schedule your first prenatal visits and tests	Make a dentist appointment
Thing plan your maternity leave	Start taking belly photos

SECOND TRIMESTER

Make appointment for second-trimester tests	Find a prenatal exercise class
Keep track of blood pressure	Shop for maternity clothes
Find out baby's gender at ultrasound	Sign up for a childbirth class
Get multiple marker screening test	Track your weight gain
Know the symptoms and risks of preeclampsia	Research baby names

THIRD TRIMESTER

Doctor exams	Learn about the stages of labor
Blood test for anemia and antibodies	Prepare for breastfeeding
Test for group B strep	Prepare house for baby
Glucose tolerance test	Make food for After baby's born
Get the Tdap vaccine	Pack hospital bag

CHAPTER 3
BIRTHING AND BUILDING A BIRTH PLAN

> "A baby fills a place in your heart that you never knew was empty." — Unknown

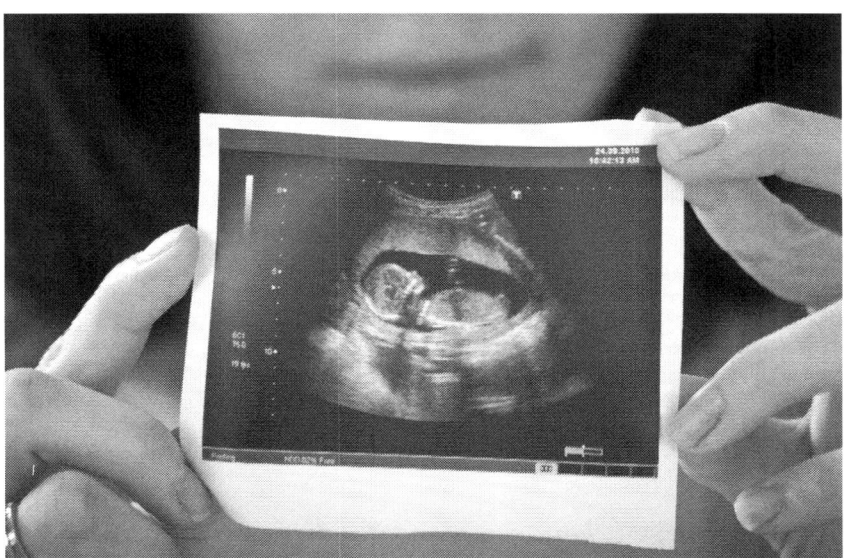

AT SOME POINT, you and your partner are going to have to discuss the ideal birthing scenario. The most common method of thinking is that the only way to give birth is to show up at the hospital, and either push the baby out vaginally, or have the baby surgically birthed by cesarean section. This isn't the case, and there are a variety of ways to give birth that will allow for a safe and comfortable delivery, depending on the desires of you and your partner. Mom needs to feel secure and comfortable when giving birth, so listen closely to her needs and desires regarding the birth.

WHERE TO DELIVER

The Hospital

The hospital is one of the most common places that women will plan to give birth. Birth is, though very natural, a major medical procedure. The body goes through incredible changes, and for some, it can be traumatic if something goes wrong. For many, the hospital is the preferred place to be for delivery so that, should anything go wrong, they are already in a medical center that is immediately prepared to intervene in any emergency scenario.

Within the hospital, you will have medical doctors (MDs) and in some, registered midwives who will supervise and assist in the birth. Typically, the hospital is equipped with special rooms for labor and maternity. These will come with varying levels of comfort; some are equipped with large comfortable chairs, while others have birthing tubs and other amenities to provide comfort and the ideal birthing scenario for mothers. Before choosing the hospital that will become the place your child is born, arrange for a tour, and consider things like the distance from home, how long it will take to get there from locations like your home or work, and the kinds of amenities that will be available to your partner as she brings your child into the world.

The downside when considering a hospital birth is that there is a significantly higher chance of unwanted medical intervention if the birth isn't moving along to the doctor's liking. While the doctor absolutely does have your health and safety in mind, you have to consider that they're busy within the hospital, and work long hours—this could mean that they might rush the labor, and try to move quickly onto the next patient, or get out after an already long day. If they can see that artificial hormones will make labor go faster, they may decide to use them, rather than just allowing the body to perform as it needs to. It's best to have a conversation with your doctor at a regularly scheduled visit well ahead of the birth.

Home

Home births are another option, especially for those who are uncomfortable with hospital births. If you and your partner choose a home birth, consider finding a registered midwife who will be able to supervise and assist in the birth. Registered midwives come with a whole host of medical knowledge should they need to intervene, but they are also trained to assist in allowing the body to do what it needs to, without rushing the job.

On the positive side, home births mean that any number of people can be invited to the birth if the mother wants more than one or two people for support (which is the typical limit that hospitals have for labor and delivery rooms). Her comfort items are already there, and she can labor where she feels most at ease. This also negates transport to and from the hospital, and means that her preferred foods and clothing are already in reach.

The downside is that if there were to be anything wrong that is outside of the care a midwife can provide, you'll likely have to rush to a hospital. Home births aren't recommended unless you've had a low-risk pregnancy overall.

Birthing Centers

Birthing centers often provide the best of hospital and home deliveries to the mother—the setting is far more comfortable than a hospital, and is specialized to labor and delivery, and if there aren't medical professionals on hand ready to intervene if necessary, the birthing center is typically quite close to local hospitals. There is no shortage of support for laboring women in a birthing center, in the form of midwives and doulas alike. (Doulas are not medical professionals, but are trained to assist a laboring and birthing mother through the process.) A birthing center can provide assistance in any way except for a c-section, which is the principal reason a mother might be transferred from the birthing center to the local hospital. If the pregnancy is high risk, a birthing center isn't recommended.

METHODS OF BIRTHING

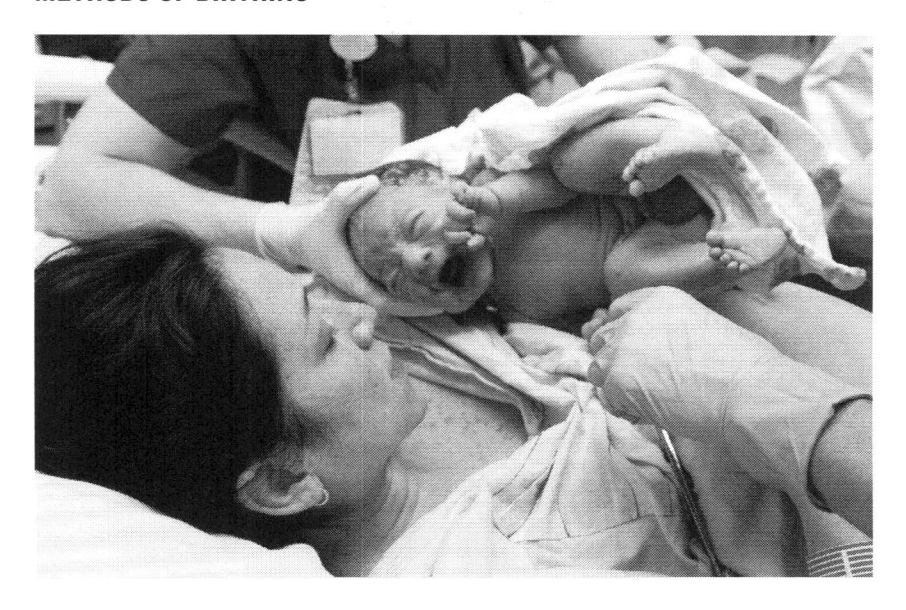

When the time comes to push, Mom might not have the utmost control over the exact method of birth she uses. This is going to depend heavily on the circumstances and the health of her pregnancy. As long as she is having a healthy pregnancy and the birth moves according to plan, she should be able to have the birth the way she desires.

Unassisted Vaginal Delivery

The unassisted vaginal delivery is the "all natural" approach. This means that Mom isn't using any kind of medication, whether it's for pain relief or to make labor move along more quickly. While a doctor, midwife, or doula may be present, the goal is for these professionals to not intervene, but to simply be there for support, and of course, to catch the baby as it enters the world. This type of birth can be held in the hospital, in a birthing center, or in the home.

The Bradley Method is often the preferred method taught and used by midwives. The course for the Bradley Method takes place over 12 weeks, teaching breathing, pain management, and nutrition that go along with caring for yourself and your partner through the end of the pregnancy. They also teach what to expect when the baby arrives, and how to best care for yourselves as you care for your little bundle of joy.

Water births are one method of unassisted childbirth that can help to make Mom more comfortable as she labors and pushes. Many birthing centers and some hospitals have tubs that are available for use, and a small pool or tub can be arranged in the home for home births. The warm water helps to soothe the mother through her contractions, and also allows for you to get into the tub with her to assist with the birth. A good-sized tub or pool helps the mother to get into more comfortable and natural positions to labor and deliver as comfortably as she can.

Lamaze can be used in both assisted and unassisted deliveries as a way to calm the body using calming, regulated breathing. The Lamaze method teaches breathing strategies, self-comfort, and soothing techniques to get you through the pain of labor. Lamaze is taught in a series of classes, teaching both Mom and her partner how to work together in getting through the birthing process as smoothly as possible, as well as teaching both partners what to be looking for and expecting when labor does begin. Typically, you should be starting Lamaze classes in the second trimester, as it does take time to learn and master the skills taught.

Assisted Delivery

Sometimes, the baby needs a little bit of help making their entrance into the world. If that is the case, the following methods may be what your medical professional recommends to help the process along so that you're holding your baby sooner than later, or they may utilize the method to help a baby that's in distress if labor doesn't progress as it should.

Amniotomy is a procedure that helps with "breaking the water" to encourage the hormone production that kickstarts labor. This may happen if the due date is long overdue, or if you're at a point in your pregnancy where a doctor is looking to help encourage labor to begin. The procedure involves using a small plastic hook to puncture a hole in the amniotic sac, releasing the fluids to encourage labor hormones to begin.

Cesarean Section starts by numbing the lower body through the use of an epidural administration of pain relief medications. The needle is inserted so that the medication can be administered around the spinal cord. After the medication has been administered, the mother may feel some pressure, but no pain from labor or the surgery.

During a c-section procedure, a horizontal incision is made just above the pelvic bone so that the surgeon can access the uterus. The baby (or babies) is then removed through this incision. Following the removal of the baby, the placenta is removed and the uterus cleared before stitching the incisions closed. Some surgeons may use staples on the external incision.

A c-section may be used or recommended for several reasons. If there is an emergency—such as the baby being in distress, the umbilical cord exiting before the baby does, or labor isn't progressing—the doctor may move forward with the c-section. A doctor may recommend a c-section in scenarios where the pregnancy involves multiple babies, the baby is in the breech position (meaning the head is upwards rather than downwards towards the birth canal, and repositioning was unsuccessful), or the baby is too large to pass through the pelvic canal. Placental abruption, where the placenta has separated from the uterine wall, and placenta previa, where the placenta is covering the opening to the cervix, may also be reasons why a doctor will call for a c-section to be performed. In the past, a c-section was also recommended to mothers who had previously had c-sections, but this isn't always necessary or mandated anymore.

Episiotomy incisions happen if the baby is stuck, or if there is any need to widen the canal so that the baby can more easily be born, especially if they are worried about the baby being under duress. The episiotomy is an incision placed along the perineum, or the tissue between the vaginal entrance and the anus, the incision often directed away from the anus. An episiotomy may heal more easily than a tear, since there will be a straight line incision.

Forceps are one method occasionally used by doctors to help guide the baby from the birth canal. The forceps look similar to two large spoons that are used to grasp onto the baby's head and help to guide the baby through the birth canal.

Induced labor is the doctor's way of manually starting labor with the use of artificial hormones to help the labor to begin. This is typically used if there is any concern for the mother or baby's wellbeing.

Vacuum extraction uses a small, soft cup attached to the top of the baby's head to help pull the baby free. The suction is just strong enough to grasp onto the baby's head, helping the medical professional assisting in the birth to pull the baby free from the birth canal.

Vaginal Birth After Cesarean (VBAC)

If this isn't your partner's first child, there is the possibility that they may have had a cesarean before. Depending on how the previous cesarean was performed, she may still be a candidate for a VBAC. As long as the previous c-section incision was done horizontally and the baby is able to fit through the pelvis, there is a likely chance that vaginal birth is an option.

BIRTH PLANS

Your birth plan is something that may grow and develop throughout the pregnancy. This is going to be the written proposal for what should happen in the labor and delivery room. Before we get into the specifics of the birth plan, it's important to note that the birth plan should be viewed as a guide for the preferred method of birth. It can be subject to change at any moment depending on the health of the baby or the mother, especially if there are extreme circumstances. Saying "no c-section" in the birth plan won't change the need for medical intervention if there is an issue during the vaginal delivery, or if there is some form of emergency that happens before the due date. Just like some moms may say they don't want any medications for pain relief during labor, if the new Mom looks at you during labor and tells you to get her the pain meds, you get her the pain meds. Birth plans are not the be all, end all. There's no way to know how labor and delivery will go, regardless if this is your first or fifth child. The most important information to have immediately visible are things like illnesses, allergies, or anything that is absolutely crucial to know.

What to Include in the Birth Plan

Think of the birth plan as the cliff notes to the ideal delivery. It shouldn't be more than a sheet, and it should hold all the crucial details related to the birth of your child. Try to keep it brief; for as much as we may want to include every single possible detail that we can think of in the "just in case" scenarios, the birth plan needs to be quickly accessible and easily scanned by a nurse, doctor, doula, or midwife that may be overseeing the birth.

- Include the basics. This should include the mother's name, your name, and the names of any other birth supports, like a doula, or any other person who should be notified that labor has begun. You should include contact information, medical information of the mother, the name and contact information of the professional who has been overseeing the pregnancy, and the name of the location where the birth is planned to take place.

- Relevant medical information. This is where you'll list any conditions the mother may have, any allergies, medications that she may be on, and any conditions that the baby may have according to tests done.
- List the birthing preferences. This pertains to the atmosphere of her labor. Does she want to be able to move about freely, be on all fours when birthing, or have an exercise ball while laboring? Does she prefer access to a tub for water birth? A quick list of preferences can help the people supervising the birth to better accommodate her preferences so that the birth can go as smoothly and trauma-free as possible.
- Intervention preferences. At what point is Mom willing to be induced with artificial hormones? Is she okay with using forceps, or does she prefer the vacuum? At what point is she willing to accept pain medication, and in what form? Does she prefer an episiotomy, or will she only allow natural tearing to happen? This section should briefly give the people overseeing the birth the information to know—aside from an emergency scenario—when the mother is willing to have them intervene, and to what degree.
- Ideal delivery. This can include the position Mom would prefer to be in, as well as preferences regarding the need for an emergency cesarean. Who should be in the room with her? How would she like the after birth details altered if she does need an emergency surgery?
- After birth details. This is where it should be listed who is preferred to be cutting the cord, what method of feeding was chosen by the parents, and the ideal

handling of the newborn upon delivery. This can mean being immediately placed on Mom's chest, or put on her belly to be allowed to crawl naturally to her breast. Some parents may prefer the baby have a moment to be wiped off and checked over before being passed to Mom or Dad, and have their own preferences regarding skin-to-skin contact. Newborn procedures such as antibiotic eye drops and the vitamin K shot should also be listed. Would you like them done right away, after the family has a moment to rest, or would you prefer to opt out?

- If Mom plans to breastfeed, she should also make note if she'd like a lactation consultant there right away. Despite the fact that breastfeeding is the most natural thing for feeding infants, it isn't all that easy for many moms, and a lactation consultant can be of enormous benefit. If she isn't planning to breastfeed, she should make note of the types of help she will require, in terms of helping to ease the pain and production of breastmilk. You may also choose to list if you'd like a pacifier presented to the child right away.

Take Action

Create your birth plan:

CHAPTER 4
PREPARING FOR THE WORST

> "Hoping for the best, prepared for the worst, and unsurprised by anything in between."
>
> — Maya Angelou

IF YOU'RE anything like me, you like to prepare for the worst, but hope for the best. While we typically anticipate a healthy pregnancy—especially if your partner is a healthy person—it can be very difficult for us to envision that these things can happen.

MISCARRIAGES AND STILLBIRTH

A miscarriage is often traumatic and devastating to the parents who have lost a child that they were looking forward to. Miscarriage is categorized as a sudden or spontaneous loss of the pregnancy, happening before the twentieth week of pregnancy. It's a natural response, especially for the mother, to feel that the miscarriage was their 'fault.' A miscarriage can sometimes be triggered by an accident or trauma, but otherwise, it's typically caused through the embryo or fetus not developing the way it should, and the body recognizing that this would-be infant won't be viable or survive the pregnancy. Putting blame on yourself or your partner isn't a healthy way to grieve, and it isn't an accurate train of thought to follow.

The symptoms of a miscarriage are pretty difficult to miss, especially in the later weeks of the first trimester and early second trimester. There may be spotting and bleeding to start, followed by severe cramping. After the cramping, there will be fluid and potentially fetal tissue that passes through the vaginal canal. If you manage to collect any of the fetal tissue, put it into a clean container to be brought to your local hospital or health care provider, so it can be analyzed for exactly why the miscarriage happened. This might give you insight on not only why it happened, but how to prevent a future miscarriage to the best of your ability.

Stillbirth is characterized by a loss of pregnancy after the twentieth week of pregnancy. While there are many cases of stillbirth that medical professionals cannot find a reason for, sometimes it comes down to the fetus not fully developing areas that they need to survive. It may be based on infection, chronic health conditions found within the mother, genetic and chromosomal abnormalities, or placental irregularities or problems.

If you and your partner do go through a miscarriage or stillbirth, please seek therapy from a professional to help you grieve the loss in a healthy manner.

ECTOPIC PREGNANCY

In a standard, healthy pregnancy, once the egg is fertilized it will latch onto the lining of the uterus. This will give the embryo plenty of room to grow and develop into a healthy fetus. In the case of an ectopic pregnancy, the egg instead takes up residence in other cavities of the uterus, most often in the fallopian tube. Unfortunately, an ectopic pregnancy is not viable, and the fertilized egg cannot be manually moved to where it needs to be. Due to the danger that an ectopic pregnancy can present, an ectopic pregnancy must be terminated.

It is incredibly difficult to know that the pregnancy is ectopic without the use of an ultrasound; the pregnancy tests will come up normal, and while the pregnancy is still new, the developing embryo will have room to grow for a short period of time. Light bleeding can be one symptom, as well as shoulder pain and the need to have frequent bowel movements. This is dependent on where the blood is coming from, and which nerves are being affected by the ectopic pregnancy. If there are symptoms like severe abdominal pain, fainting, or shock, get your partner to a doctor immediately. A ruptured fallopian tube can lead to death, and needs to be treated as soon as possible.

There is no way to really prevent an ectopic pregnancy. Some things may help, like limiting the number of sexual partners, to decrease the risk of infection and pelvic inflammation. Quitting smoking can also reduce this risk, but apart from this, there's no way to anticipate or prevent the fertilized egg getting stuck somewhere it shouldn't be.

INFERTILITY

Infertility is categorized by the inability to get pregnant after 12 months of consecutive unprotected sex. The source of the infertility can come from either partner for a vast range of reasons. There may be hormonal imbalances, issues based on drug, alcohol, or nicotine consumption, or other health problems that could potentially be resolved through medical intervention and lifestyle changes. In some cases, it may also be based on a genetic disorder, sometimes making it impossible or nearly impossible to get pregnant, especially without medical intervention. If you and your partner have been trying for longer than a year to get pregnant without success, it is recommended that you are both seen by a fertility specialist, often recommended through your primary healthcare physician.

If you are being troubled by infertility, and none of the treatments and lifestyle changes recommended by your doctor or specialist are working, the following treatments may be considered as the next step.

Intrauterine Insemination (IUI)

Also called artificial insemination, this process is sometimes known as the "Turkey Baster Method." The woman may be put onto medications or treatments to encourage her body to ovulate, followed by the manual depositing of the semen collected, to encourage a pregnancy to happen. This is often the process used when the issue is a low sperm count, or the motility of the sperm is quite low. Especially if the couple cannot find an explanation for exactly why they've been struggling to conceive, intrauterine insemination is often suggested as the first course of action if "doing it the old-fashioned way" isn't working for you.

In Vitro Fertilization (IVF)

In vitro fertilization is the process of creating an embryo outside of the body in a lab setting. This involves the extraction of mature egg cells from the ovary via a needle, and fertilizing the egg with the sperm provided by the father-to-be. Once there is a viable embryo produced, it is then implanted into the uterus to hopefully become a successful pregnancy. IVF is a very expensive procedure; there are a variety of drugs and hormones that need to be used over a period of weeks or even months in hopes to achieve a viable, successful pregnancy.

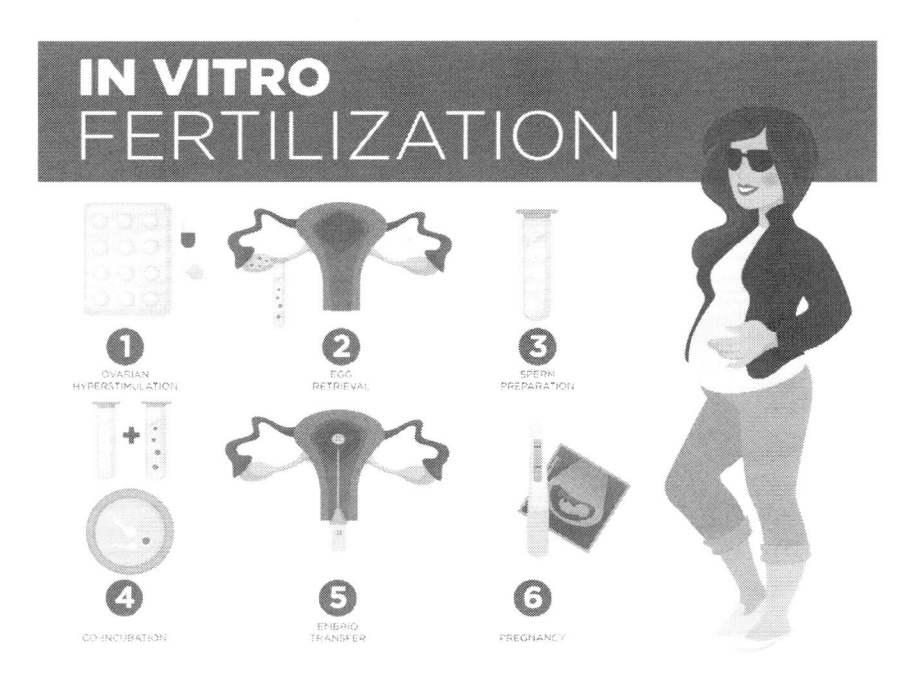

Surrogacy

If the issue that is causing the infertility is a 'hostile' environment within the uterus, or other issues that prevent your partner from successfully carrying an embryo or fetus to term, surrogacy is another option available to couples attempting to expand their family. In many cases, the couple may essentially go through the IVF process, but instead of the embryo being implanted into the uterus of the provider of the egg cell, the embryo is implanted into another healthy uterus for the baby to be carried to term.

POSSIBLE PREGNANCY COMPLICATIONS

While we all hope for a healthy, uncomplicated pregnancy, there are several different disorders that may develop during pregnancy. Contrary to popular belief, pregnancy can be very hard on the human body, so it is crucial to know what you're up against should your partner develop any of these medical disorders or problems.

Anxiety and Depression

Not only is pregnancy a time of swift hormonal changes, it's also one of the biggest changes a person or family can make in their lives. When you combine these things, depression and anxiety can easily begin during pregnancy. If anxiety or depression do begin, it is encouraged that Mom starts visiting a therapist or psychiatrist. There are some medications that can combat the symptoms of depression and anxiety during pregnancy that are safe to use while pregnant, but some pregnant mothers largely benefit from having a therapist to do talk therapy with, in place of medications. If the symptoms of anxiety or depression do occur, it should be mentioned at the next prenatal checkup with your physician. They can recommend a doctor that suits your needs and who specializes in treating pregnant women.

Breech Birth

In the earlier stages of pregnancy, the baby can be facing any which way they feel like, simply due to the fact that there is so much room for them to easily move about. As the pregnancy draws to a close, the baby should get into its birthing position, with their head downwards. When a baby is in a breech position, it means that their head is up towards Mom's rib cage. This can present all kinds of challenges and dangers when it comes time to proceed with the birth. If the baby isn't successfully turned around by the time the baby is due, the medical professional supervising the pregnancy may recommend that a c-section is done to minimize the risk of injury or mortality.

Fetal Problems

We can never predict how a fetus will develop, and if there will be issues with organ development. While some issues may be resolved with intrauterine surgeries, others may cause the child to not be viable, or to require surgery after being born. Any fetal issues in development will be discussed with you at length by your doctor. They will go over the details of the condition, cover any options, and what to expect. For the vast array of fetal problems that can possibly arise, they really aren't as frequent as the medical dramas may lead you to believe.

Gestational Diabetes

Gestational diabetes occurs when a woman who previously did not have diabetes develops the condition during her pregnancy. This is often brought on due to the fluctuation and changes in her hormones affecting the production of insulin hormones from the pancreas. Developing gestational diabetes can mean that the risk of cesarean section birth is higher—due to the fetus growing too large to be birthed vaginally—as well as the possibility of developing preeclampsia. Gestational diabetes can be managed through alterations in diet and exercise, as well as medical intervention to help the body with the insulin that the body is failing to produce properly.

High Blood Pressure

Women who experience their blood pressure suddenly spiking higher during pregnancy develop a condition called gestational hypertension. When pregnant, women increase their blood volume, and if combined with narrowing arteries, blood carrying the oxygen and nutrients that the baby needs may have a difficult time reaching the placenta. If the baby is deprived of oxygen, growth can slow down significantly. Some women need to begin using medication to control blood pressure, and if they've developed gestational hypertension, they will be very closely monitored for the symptoms of preeclampsia, which we'll look at in more detail soon. Typically, a woman will develop gestational hypertension after the 20-week mark in her pregnancy, but it will typically resolve itself after the baby's delivery.

Hyperemesis Gravidarum

While morning sickness might last for a few weeks for some, hyperemesis gravidarum is the persisting of morning sickness into the second, and sometimes even the third trimester. There isn't a known reason for this condition, but those who are affected by the disorder may need to go into the hospital for an IV of fluids and nutrients to replace what they aren't getting because of the inability to keep down food and fluids.

Infections

Infections include, but aren't limited to, sexually-transmitted infections which can endanger both Mom and baby. At varying points of the pregnancy, she may be tested to make sure that she is clear from sexually transmitted disease, as well as making sure there are no bacterial infections that could be transmitted to the baby, and potentially harm them both. Any changes in discharge consistency, color, or pain in the region should be immediately checked on by a medical professional to rule out infection, and treat the infection if there is one present.

Iron Deficiency Anemia

While pregnant, a woman's blood volume increases significantly. This can sometimes lead to iron deficiency anemia, where iron—needed for the red blood cells to carry oxygen where it needs to go—is lacking. This can result in regularly feeling fatigued and weak, sometimes even looking pale, struggling with shortness of breath, and feeling faint. Iron supplements can help with this, but if they don't appear to be

Placenta Previa

Placenta previa is a condition characterized by the placenta covering part or all of the cervical opening. During the second and third trimesters, placenta previa may cause some bleeding, which may lead to the professional supervising the pregnancy suggesting bed rest through the end of the pregnancy to minimize the risk of harm to Mom and baby. If the bleeding is too heavy, there may be a need for Mom to be hospitalized for the remainder of the pregnancy. If there are problems with the placenta, a doctor will often recommend that a c-section should be done in order to best care for the health of Mom and baby.

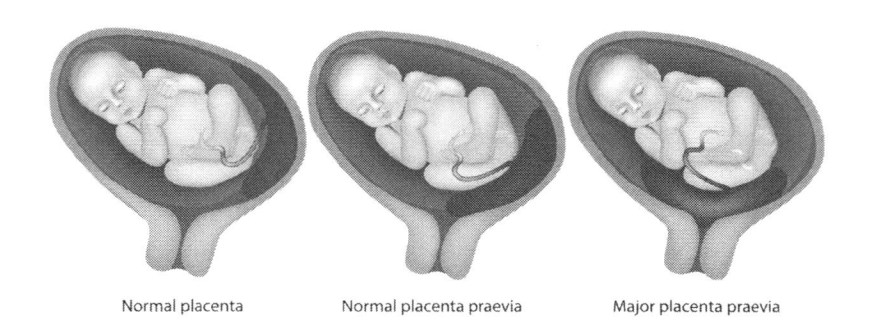

Normal placenta   Normal placenta praevia   Major placenta praevia

Placental Abruption

During a typical healthy pregnancy, the placenta is connected to the uterine lining so that the baby can get the necessary oxygen and nutrients to thrive and develop as it should. A placental abruption means that the placenta has actually separated itself from the inner lining, depriving the baby of what it needs. Abruption can come in varying levels of severity, and can cause tenderness through the abdomen and uterus, cramping, and bleeding. While minor and moderate abruption might require bed rest and supervision, severe enough placental abruption can result in the baby needing to be delivered earlier than anticipated.

Preeclampsia

The cause for preeclampsia isn't well understood by the medical community, but the disorder itself is the onset of high blood pressure after the second half of pregnancy. There are a number of risk factors that may lead to preeclampsia, such as pre-existing conditions like lupus, pre-existing high blood pressure, kidney disease, and diabetes. If this isn't her first pregnancy and she had preeclampsia in a previous pregnancy, Mom may be considered at risk of preeclampsia for this pregnancy. She may also be classified as high risk for preeclampsia if she is above the age of 35, considered obese, or is currently carrying multiple babies.

Preeclampsia is characterized by swelling in the face and extremities, high blood pressure, dizziness, headaches, and blurry vision. In extreme cases, it can lead to seizures, when it is then categorized as eclampsia. If Mom is diagnosed with preeclampsia or eclampsia, the only known way to cure the condition is to deliver the baby. This may require a preterm delivery, and if this is the case, the doctor will weigh the risks and benefits in her individual case. The decision will be based on the risks of maintaining the pregnancy in terms of the health of both mother and baby, weighed against the risks to the baby and mother of a preterm birth.

Preterm Labor

If Mom goes into labor before she reaches 37 weeks of pregnancy, it is considered preterm labor. If there are already health risks involved in the pregnancy, a doctor may sometimes recommend a preterm delivery if they believe the child to be viable and the pregnancy has become too high risk. Lung and brain development isn't complete until the final weeks, so an NICU stay may be necessary for preterm deliveries.

Preterm labor may be brought on by infections, traumatic injury, shortened cervix, or previous preterm labor instances. There are a couple ways that preterm labor can be slowed or stopped: namely, cervical cerclage, which is a surgical manner of closing the cervix to keep the baby in place, or the administration of progesterone to slow and stop labor.

Urinary Tract Infection

During pregnancy, the risk of urinary tract infections is increased due to hormone changes and the bacteria that can thrive in this environment. The infection can affect the urethra, bladder, and even kidneys, and should be treated quickly. If UTIs continue to be a common occurrence, there may be a need for medical intervention to treat the infection regularly. If a urinary tract infection goes too long without treatment, it can result in preterm labor or a low birth weight.

SCREENINGS AND TESTS

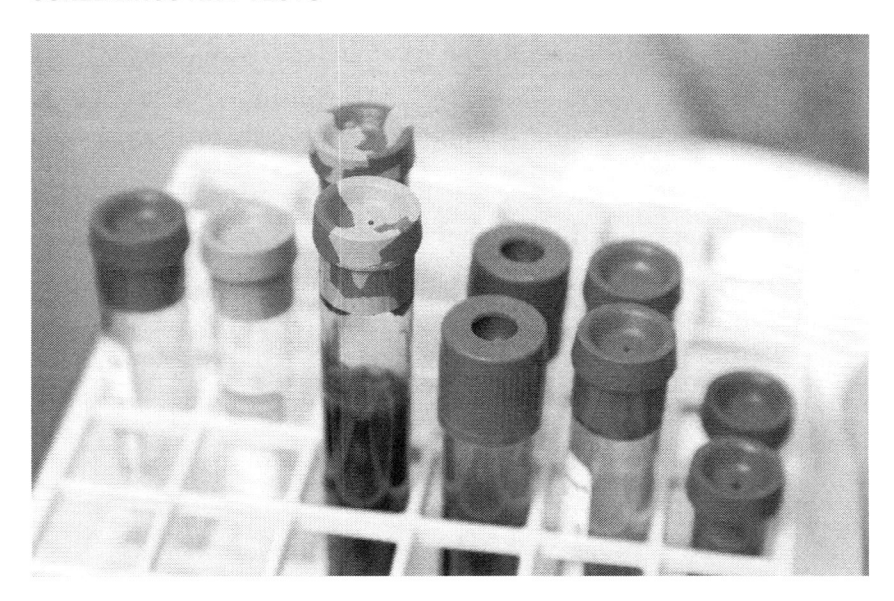

Throughout the pregnancy, there will be a variety of screenings and tests that Mom will go through. Some will be routine, whereas others will be optional screenings that you can choose with your partner whether they're necessary.

First Trimester

- **Blood Workups** - This will test for a variety of things: the pregnancy hormone hCG, any blood-borne sexually transmitted diseases, blood type and Rh factor, immunity to various diseases, and potential vitamin D deficiency. Depending on the result of this blood test, your healthcare provider may recommend other screening.

- **Chorionic Villus Sampling (CVS)** - In the case that you have a family history of genetic disorders, are over the age of 35, or if other tests have come back inconclusive, you may be recommended for CVS. This involves taking a small sample of the chorionic villi that protrude from the placenta. These resemble fingers, and are very small, but are packed with genetic information about the baby. Genetic disorders and other abnormalities will be easily found within the information of the sample, to give you an idea of what conditions your child is likely to have or is susceptible to.
- **Noninvasive Prenatal Testing (NiPT)** - Noninvasive prenatal testing allows doctors to determine the likelihood of genetic disorders, but cannot confirm if the disorder is *actually* present. This test uses a basic blood draw, then identifies and analyzes the DNA that is found in Mom's blood that originates from the baby's placenta, to screen for chromosomal abnormalities. If there is anything that raises a red flag, your medical practitioner may then recommend further screening to determine if there are genetic abnormalities present.
- **Nuchal Translucency Screening (NT)** - Nuchal translucency screening is a routine procedure done with an ultrasound. Nearing the end of the first trimester, the ultrasound is used to determine the likelihood of chromosomal abnormalities or congenital heart conditions, but cannot be used to diagnose the conditions. The ultrasound measures a transparent area that sits at the base of the baby's neck called the nuchal fold, to see how much fluid has been retained in that

area. If there is a larger amount of fluid built up in the area than average, it can indicate that the baby may be at a higher likelihood for congenital heart defect and chromosomal disorders. This screening is known to often result in false positives, so if you do get a concerning screening result, don't stress until other tests are done to confirm the findings.

- **Pap Smear** - A pap smear is likely to be done at a few points during the pregnancy, not only to check for sexually transmitted diseases, but to monitor any changes in the cervix that may indicate problems in the pregnancy. This might include the shape, appearance, and location of the cervix.
- **Rh Factor Testing** - Your Rh factor is the + or - that comes with your blood type. This is determined by whether or not your red blood cells carry the Rh factor protein on them; most people do have them, resulting in a positive blood type, like A positive, B positive, etc. If you do not carry the protein, your blood type is A negative. This doesn't tend to have any impact on your daily life… until you're pregnant. If the parents have two different blood types, then the fetus can be conceived with a different blood type than Mom's. When that happens, she could be carrying antibodies that will attack the blood cells in the fetus, as they appear to be a foreign body. This testing helps determine if there needs to be any intervention to prevent the antibodies from disrupting the baby's development or affecting Mom's health.

- **Ultrasounds** - Ultrasounds are probably every parent's favorite regular screening, since it gives us an opportunity to see the baby-in-making. Ultrasounds will help your medical practitioner check on the baby's progress, as well as measure internal organs to make sure that there are no defects or problems. The ultrasound can also monitor placental positioning, cervix length, and the amount of fluids that are present within the womb, as well as giving you a sneak peak at the fetus in its natural habitat.
- **Urine Tests** - Urine testing will take place throughout the pregnancy. These are needed to test for a variety of issues like dehydration, urinary tract infections, sugar levels related to gestational diabetes, and proteins related to preeclampsia.

Second Trimester

- **Amniocentesis** - Having amniocentesis—otherwise known as an amnio—done will give you a plethora of genetic information. A needle is inserted into the uterus, and amniotic fluid is drawn into the syringe to be sent for genetic testing. Because it is gathered from the fluid that has been circulating through the fetus, it is rich with genetic information. This will give access to knowledge on all chromosomal conditions and potential deficits, so that parents can be better informed. As a nice cherry on top, it can also provide the sex of the baby, so if you don't want to know, make sure it's noted!
- **Glucose Screening** - The glucose screening is how medical practitioners will test for gestational diabetes. There are a few variations on the test depending on what your practitioner prefers, but they all boil down to a similar procedure. When Mom shows up for her appointment, she'll be given a glucose drink—usually flavored like orange soda, but flat and with the consistency of a light syrup. After some time, usually an hour, she'll have blood drawn to test the glucose levels in her blood. This will ensure that the pancreas is still producing insulin as it should be.
- **Quad Screen** - The quad screen is yet another blood test Mom will go through. This one will test four different chemicals that pass through her bloodstream as the blood cycles through her body and the placenta.
- - Alpha-Fetoprotein (AFP), which is a protein produced by the baby.

- - Estriol, a hormone in the estrogen family that is produced by both the baby and the placenta.
- - Human chorionic gonadotropin (hCG), which is the pregnancy hormone that is also detected in urine during a positive pregnancy test. This hormone is produced by the placenta.
- - Inhibin A, which is another hormone produced by the placenta.
- The quad screen will indicate whether your baby *may* have any neural tube defects or chromosomal conditions. This won't give a definitive answer, but will let doctors know if they need to do more in-depth testing.

Third Trimester

- **Biophysical Profile** - If the pregnancy is considered healthy and low risk, chances are that Mom won't need this one. The biophysical profile is another ultrasound that will focus on the baby's motion, breathing, the progress of their organs, and the amount of amniotic fluid. This profile screening is a way to check in on the baby to make sure that the pregnancy is progressing safely.
- **Group B Strep Test** - Group B strep is a bacteria that, while perfectly fine when found in adults, can lead to serious health complications if transmitted to the infant during birth. If Mom tests positive for this bacteria, she will be given a course of antibiotics to clear the infection before the baby is born.

- **Nonstress Test** - A nonstress test is administered for a variety of reasons: Mom may have preeclampsia or other gestational complications, the baby appears small in comparison to their gestational age, or you've surpassed your due date significantly, and it's time to check in on the baby. The baby will simply be monitored in a nonstress environment to ensure that everything is still in line with health parameters.

CHAPTER 5
FIRST TRIMESTER

> "Having a kid is like falling in love for the first time when you're 12, but every day."
>
> – Mike Myers

THE FIRST TRIMESTER is a rollercoaster time period, but an exciting one! Trying to conceive is an emotional journey, so finally reaching the point where your partner is now forming your tiny life in her womb is something to celebrate. The first trimester is made up of the first 12 weeks of pregnancy, and can be a whirlwind time.

EMBRYO DEVELOPMENT

- Fertilized
- Zygote and first cleavage
- 4 cell
- Morula
- Blastocyst
- Embryo

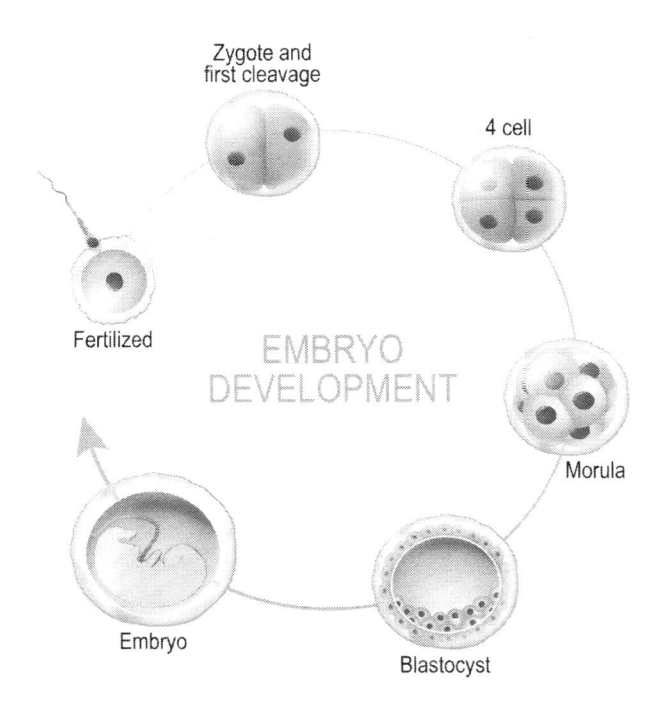

WEEK 1 & 2

This time period actually starts at the first day of Mom's period, so the first couple of weeks are pretty uneventful in terms of gestation. The first week is the menstrual period where the lining of the uterus is shed from the past month, beginning the cycle of creating a fresh new uterine lining to support an implanted fertilized egg. As a matter of fact, the day you're looking for is the last day of the second week, approximately the 14th day of the cycle when the ovary releases the egg, hoping to be fertilized by some lucky sperm. This fertility window opens

FIRST TRIMESTER 59

three to five days before ovulation, depending on Mom's typical cycle. Once the egg is fertilized, it'll be implanted, and you can consider yourselves pregnant!

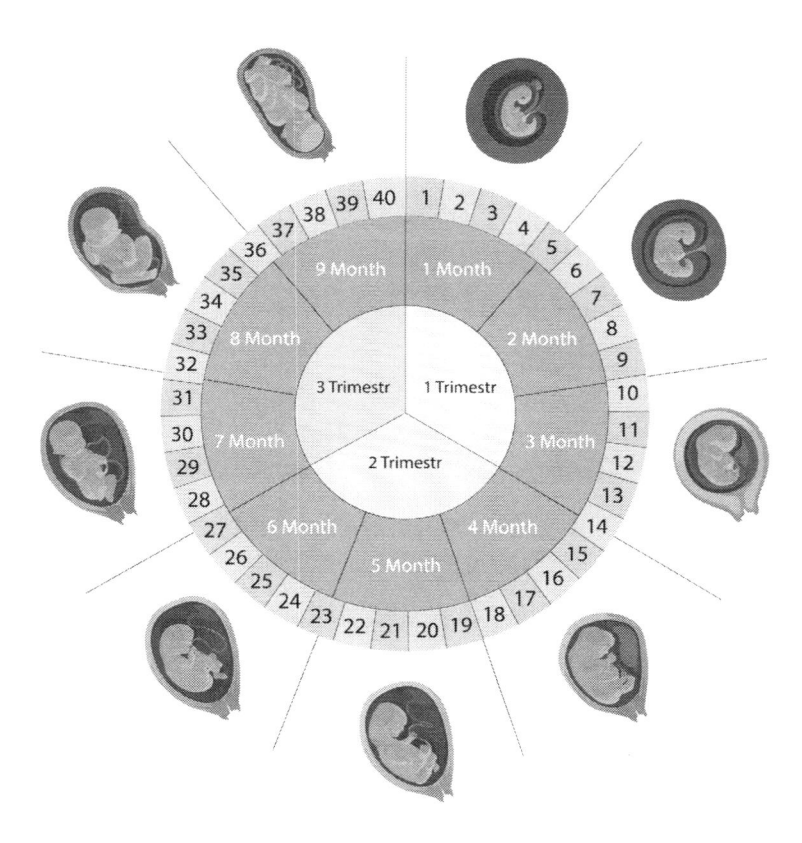

EMBRYO DEVELOPMENT

WEEK 3

Most women don't know they're pregnant at this point, and most tests won't pick up the pregnancy at this point. There are rarely any symptoms at this point. Some might notice a tiny bit of spotting or the slightest bit of cramping, but otherwise, most people don't recognize any kind of change by week three. The earliest signs of pregnancy that might possibly occur is your partner's breasts being more tender or swollen, and she may have a heightened sense of smell. Some women may experience some nausea from the shifting hormones as well. Right now, your baby is a blastocyst, which is the tiniest little cluster of multiplying cells.

WEEK 4

How is the Baby?

This week, your future baby changes from a blastocyst to an embryo. Within the uterus, the amniotic sac and placenta that will protect your baby in utero are beginning to form. If you and your partner have been actively trying to get pregnant, this may be the point, right about the time she should be missing her period, that the pregnancy should become visible on home pregnancy tests.

How is Mom?

Typically, there aren't many symptoms at this point, but this will vary person to person. Some will experience some mild pressure in or around their uterus, or may see some implantation bleeding. Others may notice symptoms like tender breasts or feeling exhausted, but it's also just as normal to notice no symptoms at all! It's easy to mistake the earliest symptoms as an oncoming menstrual period. Of course, the rapidly rising rate of the pregnancy hormones may bring along some nausea or vomiting, but not every pregnancy comes with morning sickness. Symptoms will range per person, so don't jump at every sneeze or mood swing.

How Can Dad Help?

First, bring home a pregnancy test! This is the ideal time to start testing, after all. Bear in mind that human chorionic gonadotropin (hCG), the hormone released by the placenta during pregnancy, will increase at different rates per person, so it's entirely possible to get a false negative or a very faint positive at this stage. If you do get that positive pregnancy test, it's time to make an appointment for prenatal care so that Mom and baby's health and progress can be tracked.

If your partner is experiencing any potential symptoms, treat it the same way you might help soothe period symptoms: warm compresses for cramping, ginger or ginger ale for the nausea, and caring for your partner's emotional state. If you're not sure what your partner really needs, communicate! They can tell you far better than the pages of a book, in terms of what they individually need to soothe discomfort.

If you have any major concerns about disorders like sickle cell disease and other genetic disorders, consider carrier screening. It's a simple saliva or blood test that can help you prepare if you know that yourself or your partner are carriers of any major disorders so that you can be prepared, if you so choose.

Finally, if you've gotten a positive on the pregnancy test, what your partner consumes now becomes important. Prenatal vitamins are a great thing to start now if they haven't been already. In terms of dietary needs this week, vitamin D and healthy fats are a great place to focus your energy. If she's struggling with getting the good leafy greens in due to nausea, hide them in fruit smoothies or blend them into pasta sauces. If your partner's nausea is making it difficult to eat, work with them to get them what they need.

WEEK 5

How is Baby?

Right now, your baby looks like a tadpole. The nutrients Mom is giving the baby are helping it to form its nerve passageways; this includes the brain, spinal cord, and nerves, giving the baby the appearance of having a tail. The baby's gut, heart, and lungs are also starting to form this week. These crucial organs developing means that if Mom is usually a smoker or around smokers, she should be removing herself from that smoke exposure, as well as away from alcohol consumption. Caffeine consumption should be reduced to about one or two small cups of coffee in a day, since there isn't enough known about the effects of caffeine on the baby at this time.

How is Mom?

If the pregnancy test from last week left you guessing, this week should give you something far more conclusive to go off of. Fatigue, tender breasts, nausea, and now needing to run to pee constantly are going to be the normal, expected symptoms your partner might experience. Hormones are climbing in your partner's body at an exceptional rate, so be patient with any hormonal mood swings that she may be experiencing. Food aversions may be starting to set in, making cooking and eating certain items seem impossible, so adjusting the food Mom is eating may be necessary.

How Can Dad Help?

From here on out, if you have a cat, your pregnant partner should skip cleaning the litter box. This doesn't mean get rid of the cat, as some folk legends suggest. Dealing with litter boxes and gardening without gloves can contribute to contracting an infection called toxoplasmosis, which can harm both Mom and baby. Anywhere that outdoor cats might be using as a potty is generally good for Mom to avoid if possible, including uncovered sandboxes.

Some couples find that a pregnancy journal can be great to start at this time. This will give parents and child a way to look back on the pregnancy, and creates a keepsake for the child. It's also a great time to start talking about saving money for the baby, both for baby's arrival and their future.

WEEK 6

How is Baby?

Your baby's heart is working overtime! Right now, the baby's heart rate is double yours. Baby's little face is beginning to take shape, and may even be visible in an ultrasound. Their features may only show as small dark spots on their face at this point, but they're there! Even the baby's tongue and vocal cords are forming right now, along with the ears. It won't be long until the baby will be able to hear your voice through Mom's belly. Tiny arms and legs are also budding at this point, though your baby still looks a bit like a tadpole with a tail.

How is Mom?

Mom might be feeling a little more emotional right about now. This is all pretty new, so combining the hormonal changes with the physical changes, plus the stress and nerves that can come with knowing you're really pregnant, can create a melting pot of worry. Strange dreams might come with the subconscious stress that she may be feeling right now. Worries about the baby's health, how the balance of baby and work and social life will work, if you've got the finances in place, or if you'll be good parents can all pile up and reflect in her moods.

Physically, your partner is probably feeling the need to pee a lot more often. Blood is being pushed by rising levels of hCG to her pelvic area. Odd cravings may begin to develop, fatigue and morning sickness may be in full swing, and heartburn may start to rear its ugly head, thanks to hormones relaxing the band that typically keeps stomach acids where they belong. If that wasn't enough, many women begin experiencing headaches around this point, often related to not getting enough sleep, their cravings that might be loaded with sodium or MSG, stress, being around smoke, or other factors. Take the time to find the source of the headaches so that you can get rid of them effectively.

How Can Dad Help?

Since you're still very early in the pregnancy, this is a great time to be educating yourselves in the foods that aren't safe to eat during pregnancy, or that aren't recommended to consume in high amounts. This includes foods like soft cheeses, overly processed meats, raw meats and fish, and some shellfish. Educating yourself ahead of time will mean making it easier to make a choice for food when you're out for a meal. There are lots of apps that can help you figure out if food is safe while on the go as well.

Regarding the health of Mom and baby, healthy snacks and taking short walks can be a great way to prevent the worst of the soreness that can set in from pregnancy down the road, especially if you make it a habit now. Otherwise, if your partner is showing signs of stress, offer a listening ear. Ask her if she just wants to be heard, or if she wants solutions; if she wants solutions, then you can begin looking realistically into whatever is worrying her. Otherwise, just hear her out and soothe her however works best for her, and let her know that she has your support. Do what you can to help her reduce stress if the hormones are running away with her. If there's a routine that she tends to enjoy to destress, like a warm—not hot! Extreme temperatures are bad for the baby!—bath or massage, set them up for her. Take the initiative, rather than waiting for her to ask for you to do something kind.

WEEK 7

How is Baby?

Your baby's brain is expanding like crazy this week! Roughly 100 new brain cells are generated per minute in this stage, since the energy of reproducing and growing is being focused on the head right now. The little buds that were the beginnings of arms and legs are developing more this week as well, but they still look like tiny paddles for now. Your baby's kidneys have also begun developing, and getting ready to start working on waste management; yes, the baby *does* pee in the womb!

How is Mom?

Mom's symptoms are probably fairly consistent with what she's been experiencing up to this point, except for the fact that she may have gone up a whole bra size by this point. Mom may already be experiencing the itching that comes along with stretching skin. She should build the habit early to be moisturizing areas like the hips, buttocks, breasts, legs, and belly to reduce the discomfort of stretching skin. There's also the issue of all the excess saliva. Saliva production goes wild thanks to those pregnancy hormones, as well as her acne going crazy. If Mom typically goes to the gym to work out, she only has a few more weeks where she can safely and comfortably work out her back, so she should definitely get in her exercises while she can!

How Can Dad Help?

For now, what you've been doing up to this point is what you should continue doing. Continue to offer support for the pregnancy symptoms that your partner is experiencing, listening to their worries, and communicating plans and ideas for the birth, even if it seems as though it's forever away. It can be a great idea to get a pulse on your relationship; making sure the foundations of your relationship are strong will ensure that you can both feel secure in your ability to parent and communicate with each other when things are difficult, due to sleep deprivation. It may even be fun to come up with name ideas, what your official pregnancy announcement will be, and discuss what you're excited about.

WEEK 8

How is Baby?

This week, your baby is starting to move around, although it's incredibly unlikely for you or Mom to feel the movements at this point. These movements are happening as the baby's nerves develop, causing it to twitch and move unpredictably. Meanwhile, little features like lips, eyelids, and even a tiny baby nose are starting to form. The baby is growing very quickly right now, making it easier to see its shape in ultrasounds.

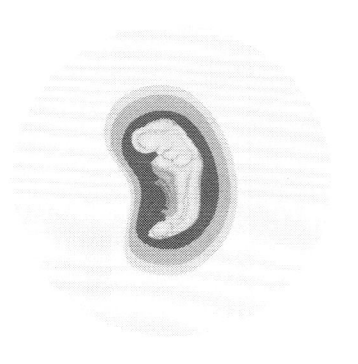

How is Mom?

Mom might be feeling the baby weight right now. While it isn't likely that she's showing yet, she's probably starting to put on a bit of weight; this is a good thing! It is crucial for her to be putting on weight throughout her pregnancy to support the baby as best she can. Having a steady supply of fruit available will also supply the fibre she needs to combat the constipation that might be setting in around this time. Alongside the fruit, Mom should be staying well hydrated.

Fatigue is also normal at this stage; she may have barely done anything that day, and still feel like she needs a nap. This could be partly due to the crazy pregnancy dreams that she might be having, as well as the energy it takes to be making the baby. Finally, she may be noticing some changes in her vaginal discharge; it may be thickening into something that looks white and creamy. As long as the change isn't drastically altering the smell and color, it's perfectly normal. It is still safe to be having sex, despite the changes in the discharge. As long as the pregnancy is healthy and she can get into a comfortable position, the changes in her discharge won't affect her ability to enjoy some one-on-one affection!

How Can Dad Help?

Keep fresh fruit stocked in the house. Make sure it's something that she feels she can eat if she is experiencing morning sickness. Especially if she's having trouble getting her veggies to stay down, keeping a rainbow fruit assortment can mean still getting the nutrition she needs to support both herself and the growing baby. Regardless of the season, keep a bottle of sunscreen around. Pregnancy can bring on melasma, a condition that causes darker hyperpigmentation of the skin. Keeping the skin protected (yes, even during the winter!) can keep this from happening.

If you're a couple that does meal planning, Mom will benefit from having smaller, more frequent meals throughout the day. Even if she's still dealing with morning sickness, having something small available when she feels like she can eat will do wonders. Especially when combined with the fatigue that comes with pregnancy, small pre-made meals that she can quickly warm up if needed can help ensure that she's eating well for both her and baby.

WEEK 9

How is Baby?

It's officially the third month of pregnancy! This is the final week that the baby is classified as an embryo, and will be moving on to its fetus stage next week. The baby's facial features, as well as tiny toes, knees, and elbows are formed and potentially visible in an ultrasound. If the baby is positioned in the right area, the heartbeat can even be heard during the ultrasound. Now that the baby is about an inch long, it'll be easier for an ultrasound technician to tell if you're having one baby, or multiples!

How is Mom?

Meanwhile, fatigue is probably kicking Mom's butt. Her body is working overtime to form the placenta that will surround and protect the baby, as well as getting baby the oxygen and nutrients that it needs to keep growing at a steady rate. Between the hormones, the fatigue, heartburn, sore breasts, and the weight gain as her uterus expands, she might be going through some hefty mood swings.

If there are any complications within the pregnancy, signs can start right around this time period. Issues like spotting and bleeding, excessive cramping in the lower back, and severe itching can all indicate that there may be something wrong.

How Can Dad Help?

For now, keep stocked up on those snacks! Keeping food down as much as possible will help Mom with the heartburn, while also keeping her and baby fed. If Mom is still feeling the fatigue, pick up the slack where she's struggling to keep up, and help her with the bigger tasks around the house. If you're looking to treat her, look into what spa treatments are available locally, and check that they are safe for pregnancy.

WEEK 10

How is Baby?

Congratulations! Your embryo has officially graduated from embryo to fetus! Your baby is going through a bunch of new changes this week. You might even be able to get a firsthand look at it, as most doctors will schedule the first ultrasound between this week and next. The baby's forehead will probably look like it has a hump, since the brain is developing and starting to bulge forward. The baby's teeth are also starting to form and harden, attaching themselves to the jaw bone. Bones are also beginning to form and harden right now, and the baby can already bend and flex their tiny arms and legs. The baby's organs are also developing, such as stomach and kidneys. If the baby is a boy, he's already started producing testosterone.

How is Mom?

As for Mom, she's about to start showing if she isn't already. Her uterus has expanded enough to start seeing some rounding in her lower belly, depending on her height, build, and weight. This outwards push could mean feeling cramping in her lower abdomen, but there's no need to panic just yet! Round ligament pain—which is going to come from the ligaments that will do some of the major lifting as the baby grows—may be setting in due to stretching right about now. While some hardly notice them, other women find the pain can almost rival their menstrual cramps.

If Mom has been experiencing mood swings, they should be coming to an end in the next few weeks, but can likely return near the end of the pregnancy. She may find that she's dealing with excessive saliva production, veins becoming more visible, some level of constipation, and the constant feeling of needing to pee. All of this is normal, and comes with the territory of fluctuating hormones and the exhaustion of building a whole human from scratch. Considering how much the baby is growing right now, she should be staying on top of taking her vitamins, especially folic acid, vitamins A through E, and iron to help with the energy levels.

Mom's clothes might also be getting tight right about now. If she doesn't already have some, it may be time for her to get some maternity pants, or some other stretchy clothes that will grow with her. Don't go too crazy on them yet though; she's still got a long way to go in terms of her changing body.

How Can Dad Help?

If the first ultrasound is this week, celebrate and enjoy it with your partner. This is the first look you're getting at the being that will be your child, so cherish the moment as much as you can. You should also discuss with your partner if you'd like to have any potential screenings done. There are a variety to choose from, and they will let you know if your baby will have any special needs or conditions that could effect their quality of life.

It's also time to start considering your budget for baby's arrival. New babies are quite expensive, so now that you're nearing the end of the first trimester, talking about savings, work schedules, and the possibility of either of you being stay-at-home or work-from-home parent is important. It should also be on the radar to discuss maternity leave and/or paternity leave between the two of you, and with your respective employers. While you don't necessarily have to do it right now, your employer will need time to find a replacement for either of you while you're gone, as well as making the time for the appointments associated with pregnancy. In Mom's case, they may also have to adjust the type of work she's doing, so that she's not putting excessive strain on her body or exposing herself to dangerous chemicals.

WEEK 11

How is Baby?

Baby is truly leaving their amphibian phase, and really embracing their new fetus stage. They're now moving about freely, doing somersaults, kicks, and stretches now that the body is starting to straighten out. Webbing that once connected the fingers and toes is now disappearing, and individual fingers and toes are visible and wiggling freely. On those fingers and toes, there are nascent nail beds, but don't worry, they won't be hardening into the nails we have for some time. They may be sharp, but they'll be fairly paper-like until after the baby is born. Even the baby's hair follicles are developing over their head and all over their body, so they can grow hair to help keep them warm when they make their entrance.

If your baby is a girl, this week her ovaries will develop. Regardless of gender, the external sex organs are beginning to develop, but they won't be distinguishable enough at this point to see clearly on an ultrasound if you're having a boy or a girl. While these organs are developing, other internal organs are starting to function. The pancreas, kidneys, and liver are all doing their jobs: making insulin, urine, and red blood cells respectively.

How is Mom?

Mom's first trimester symptoms should start tapering off at this point, only to be replaced by the second trimester symptoms. It'll be important for her to stay well hydrated to fend off constipation and leg cramping, even though it'll contribute to her needing the bathroom constantly. She may also be noticing some darkening in her skin; a line may become visible that runs through the center of her abdomen called linea nigra, as well as her areolas darkening. These color changes won't stick around forever. They typically disappear after the birth; they may linger during breastfeeding due to the hormones associated with nursing, but they'll eventually fade out and disappear.

She may also feel a little more stomach trouble, but in the form of gas and bloating. This arises from slowed digestion, thanks to those lovely hormone changes (they really are to blame for pretty much every discomfort at this point) and the shifting inside her body as the baby grows and the uterus expands. High-fiber foods and lots of water can help, as well as avoiding the foods that cause gas, if it's making her uncomfortable.

How Can Dad Help?

A babymoon is a great way to bond with your partner before the baby arrives. The second trimester is probably the ideal time if you want to travel a little bit, so start your planning now! The harsh symptoms of the first trimester are probably subsiding, and the third trimester tends to get more uncomfortable. Meanwhile, the second trimester is usually the point where most women get to really enjoy their pregnancy, so this is the best time to go on a special little vacation if you can.

WEEK 12

How is Baby?

It's the final week of the first trimester! You're a third of the way to becoming new parents now—how does it feel? If you and your partner have been worried about miscarriage, reaching the 12-week mark is a great sign, since the chances of miscarriage drop significantly now.

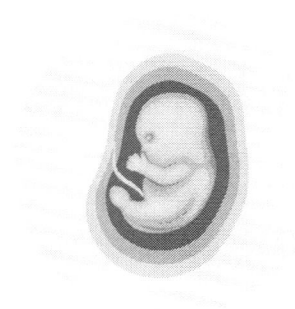

At this point, all of your baby's major organs have formed, and from this point on, the baby will be putting all of its energy into developing and growing all its parts. The organs are all functioning, with its bone marrow now working on creating white blood cells, and the intestines are getting in practice with working food through them. Right now, the baby is getting a start on making meconium, which will be their first poop. This is mostly made up of cells, bile, and various types of proteins and fats that get processed through their organs. The baby can now do things like clench their fists, and is getting way more active. While not common, some women might feel a little flutter of movement in her womb, commonly mistaken for gas rolling through the intestines. It's not likely that you'll feel anything with your hand on her belly, but that time is coming soon!

How is Mom?

While most of the harsher symptoms of the first trimester should be slowing down, hormones are doing new things in

Mom's body. One of these hormones, progesterone, can start causing dizziness, thanks to its ability to restrict and dilate blood vessels. This change in the blood vessels can even make her feel short of breath, so if dizziness or having a tough time breathing kicks in, she should take a seat and rest for a while. If she's wearing tight clothing, it can help to loosen them up and take a moments rest to gather herself. Progesterone can also drastically affect her libido, but which direction is highly dependent on the person. Some will feel their libido sink entirely due to the hormone shift, while others might not be able to get enough.

How Can Dad Help?

If you haven't already, the 16th-week ultrasound should be scheduled. Otherwise, keep the pregnancy-safe foods stocked up, and roll with the changes in Mom's libido. Especially if her libido is down, don't take it personally; she isn't in control of her hormones, and it's not likely anything to do with you. If you have any concerns, communicate with her about them. There isn't anything wrong with checking in to make sure that the relationship is stable, and that she's doing well, mentally. If the stress and anxiety that come with depression are really settling in, encourage her to speak with a therapist to help alleviate these worries from her mind.

CHAPTER 6
SECOND TRIMESTER

> "Words can not express the joy of new life." — Hermann Hesse

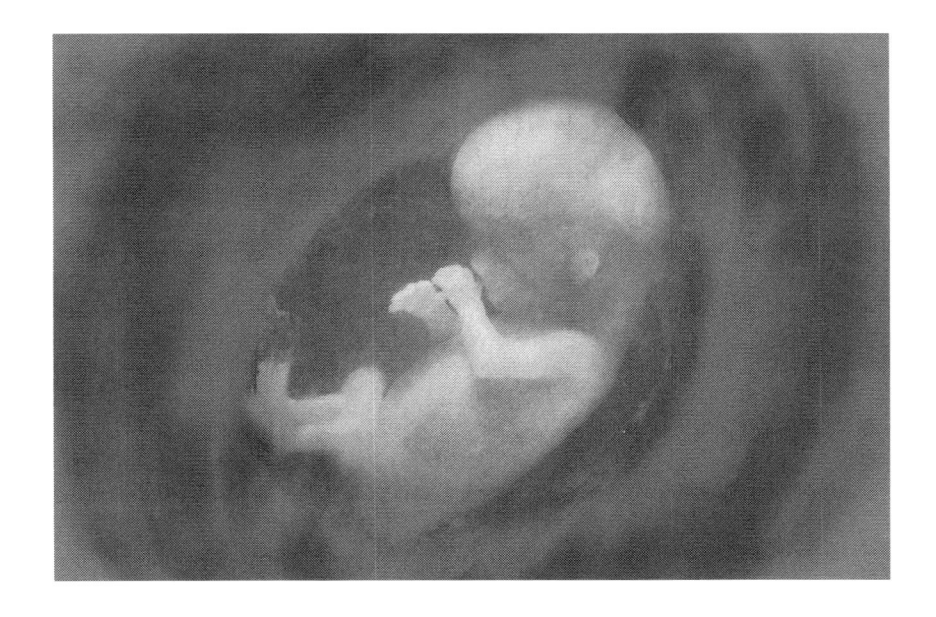

WELCOME TO THE SECOND TRIMESTER! The second trimester is where the funnest parts of pregnancy often take place, so enjoy it as much as you can. Now that Mom's worst symptoms should be starting to alleviate, you get to look forward to the amazing growing belly, the kicks, the gender reveal (if you want to know what you're having,) and all kinds of other cool moments in the pregnancy.

WEEK 13

How is Baby?

Baby is working on their vocal cords this week, getting ready for you to hear their little voice. In the vicinity, the eyelids are present, but they're still fused closed to protect their delicate eyes. They will stay this way for a while still. At the same time, bones within the skull, as well as the longer bones of the body and teeth, are becoming more dense and are hardening. This will help the baby to move more effectively, and they may even start sucking on their thumb.

Baby's intestines are also moving into the area that they will be staying long term. Before this week, the intestines were actually tucked away within the umbilical cord, but they'll start their journey into the abdominal cavity while they work on storing up their first poops. This comes from the fact that the baby is now swallowing amniotic fluid, cycling the fluid through their urinary and digestive system.

How is Mom?

Mom's appetite should return in full force right about now, which will help with the weight that she should be putting on to support the pregnancy. She's likely enjoying the break from morning sickness, and may even be sleeping a little bit better as she adjusts to the hormone changes that she's been experiencing. This can mean that she has a lot more energy than she had over the last few months.

While some symptoms are alleviating, she may still be experiencing some of the more pesky ones, like heartburn and cramping, thanks to the round ligaments stretching out. Constipation and indigestion can still be lingering, meaning she needs to keep her water intake up, and keep eating smaller, more frequent meals with a good level of fiber. Apart from this, she still needs to be taking her prenatal vitamins. Folic acid, calcium, protein, and iron are all important during this stage of the pregnancy.

An increase in vaginal discharge is also fairly standard at this point, and may not be such a bad thing if she's been experiencing a heightened libido. On the other hand, she may also be dealing with new levels of congestion, which some women experience thanks to those lovely pregnancy hormones. If she happens to be dealing with a cold at the same time, she'll need to go the all-natural route, since most cold medications aren't pregnancy safe.

How Can Dad Help?

For now, embrace the window of relief that your partner is feeling; while her libido may be up, certainly enjoy it, but get out of bed and go enjoy yourselves doing pregnancy-safe activities that you previously enjoyed doing together. Whether it's going for walks and hikes, swimming, doing something artsy, or enjoying some restaurant food instead of home cooking, enjoy the time you have where it's just the two of you. Just be careful if she's still experiencing some of the dizziness and headaches that can sometimes come with pregnancy. It's great if she has a lot more energy, but be careful about going too hard on the physical endeavors so she doesn't risk fall or injury. On the topic of food, if the morning sickness and food aversions are settling down, enjoy cooking and eating together, especially the foods that she has regained an appetite for.

WEEK 14

How is Baby?

This week, the baby's face is getting a serious workout. Because of the development going on in the brain, the baby's face is making all kinds of expressions, flexing the tiny muscles that will eventually help them smile and frown. Those spurts of movement, thanks to their developing brain, also contribute to the baby starting to move, kick, punch, and stretch more these days, even if you can't *quite* feel them at it yet.

They're also slowly growing more of the fuzzy hair that covers them from head to toe, and it will slowly become more pronounced around the head, eyebrows, and eyelashes. The hair that will grow to cover the baby's body is called lanugo, which is very fine. Think of a tiny baby otter with a thin coating of fuzzy, soft hair covering them for warmth. The baby will likely hold onto that lanugo until they're born, when they'll shed the fuzz and opt for clothes and smooth baby skin. The purpose of the lanugo is to keep the baby warm while their baby fat comes in. While the baby's body is developing, the priority isn't necessarily putting on baby fat, but putting the energy towards growing and developing muscles, bones, and organs.

Possibly the most exciting development that your baby is going through right now is the full formation of external sex organs. For now, it might be a bit difficult to see in the ultrasounds, since baby is still quite small—roughly the size of your fist. In just a few more weeks, it will become much easier to see on the ultrasound if you're hoping to know your little one's gender.

How is Mom?

This is likely a very exciting time if Mom hasn't been showing a whole lot up to this point. By week 14, the baby bump is well underway for most, so if she's not seeing it as much as she'd like, that bump will be popping up in no time! She's also going to be enjoying some shinier and even thicker hair. If she already had thick hair to begin with, she may consider getting it thinned out at some point just for the sake of comfort. Her nails may also be growing in stronger and longer than before; there are upsides to the pregnancy hormones after all.

Despite feeling better, the round ligament pains might be coming in with a vengeance right now, since she's starting to show more. Her body knows it's about to expand a lot more around the middle, so it's doing everything to get those ligaments ready. If she hasn't already been working on strengthening her pelvic floor muscles, some pelvic muscle exercises will help her in the long run as the baby grows. If the round ligament pains are really bothering her, a warm or cool compress can help. If they're really uncomfortable, maternity belts and spider tapes can help to relieve some of the pain, as well as gentle massage.

Finally, she may be experiencing something sort of strange that nobody tends to mention; bleeding gums. Pregnancy gingivitis isn't uncommon, and can come about because of hormone changes, as well as being increasingly sensitive to bacteria. Increasing the amount that she's brushing and flossing can be a big help in minimizing the effects of pregnancy gingivitis, as well as still going on regular dentist visits. Especially after dealing with morning sickness, visiting a dentist can help negate any long-term effects that her teeth deal with during pregnancy.

How Can Dad Help?

Both of you should be working hard to stay healthy right about now. Depending on what time of the year you and your partner conceived, you may be going through cold and flu season right about now. Washing hands, using hand sanitizer, and generally keeping a distance from sick people should be high on both of your priority lists. Right now, Mom's immune system is way more susceptible to illness, so commit yourself to germ and virus destruction. If you happen to catch something, keep your distance and maybe sleep in the guest room or on the couch. If

Mom happens to catch a cold or other virus, get her to a doctor who can prescribe pregnancy-appropriate antibiotics or medications.

WEEK 15

How is Baby?

If you could see into baby's little home in the uterus this week, they might look like something out of a sci-fi movie. The baby's skin is formed, but for now, it's still very thin, meaning that you could easily see through it and peek at all of its blood vessels. The skeleton is continuing to harden, and is now hard enough that, if you were to x-ray your baby (not recommended to do so though, as the radiation is not good for a fetus), you would be able to see a little skeleton forming. As the skull hardens, the eyes and ears are migrating into the places they should be. Soon, they will arrive where they are going to be staying, and your baby's face will be officially formed.

The baby is also poking its tongue out these days, tasting the amniotic fluid. That may sound strange, but if you had brand new taste buds, you'd probably be pretty excited to taste everything in your environment too! The most interesting thing is, in a way, the baby can taste what Mom eats through the amniotic fluid. It's not in the way you think; if she eats a carrot, the amniotic fluid doesn't become carrot flavored. The compounds within the foods, like amino acids, proteins, glucose, fats, and minerals can make their way into the amniotic fluid, giving the baby a sense of the food that is available in the outside world. If Mom eats a shawarma, the baby may not taste exactly what a shawarma is like, but they can still taste some of the compounds that give food their flavor. A fetus in utero can even respond to presumably favorite or disliked foods, depending on their reactions to certain foods.

The baby is getting plenty of practice in for when they make their grand arrival into the world. They've started not only doing fetal aerobics, but also practicing skills like sucking, swallowing, and even breathing so that their reflexes and muscles are prepared for life outside of the womb. These fetal aerobics of punching, kicking, rolling, and stretching may mean that very, very soon, Mom might be feeling the baby move, if she hasn't already. You might struggle to feel the baby with your hand on her belly, but internally, most women compare the early feeling of the kicks to popcorn popping in the belly, lots of gas moving through the belly, or someone flicking her from the inside.

How is Mom?

Physically, the symptoms Mom has been experiencing going into trimester number two should still continue. Bouts of round ligament pain are standard, and of course, paying extra attention to her teeth and gums right now is a must. While she's coping with her pregnancy symptoms, her weight gain should be fairly steady; roughly four pounds or about 2 kilograms a month is the average. It's okay if she's a little above or below the average monthly net weight gain. Every Mom is different, with varying metabolisms and body types, so if her weight gain is off by a few pounds, it's nothing to worry too much about, unless otherwise indicated by the doctor.

Of the stranger pregnancy symptoms, Mom may also be dealing with nosebleeds. The hormones that have caused her to feel congested, combined with all of the extra blood that is in her body these days, are to blame for this one. These hormones are going to make her nasal cavities far more sensitive, and may thin the membranes just enough that nosebleeds can happen. This is normal, but if it seems that she's bleeding an awful lot and you're concerned, you can always talk to your medical practitioner just to make sure everything is okay.

Does Mom seem a little more disorganized lately? This may be a sign of "pregnancy brain" kicking in. Mom's brain actually does change during pregnancy, to the point that in the third trimester, the brain will lose brain cell volume. This is temporary, but it's the reason that Mom starts forgetting appointments, misplaces things more often than she used to, and may even forget what she's talking about mid sentence. This early into pregnancy brain, it's less to do with decreased brain cell volume, and more to do with the combination of altered sleeping, hormones raging, and an overall feeling of brain fog. If she's struggling with pregnancy brain, it may be a good idea to start using her calendar and notes apps on her phone (provided that she can keep track of where she left it.)

How Can Dad Help?

There are two important things to discuss right now; one, if your partner is at risk for preeclampsia, she should speak to her medical practitioner if a low dose or baby aspirin will be appropriate for her to take, to help lower the risk of high blood pressure setting in. Two, it's time to discuss whether or not amnio, short for amniocentesis, is a test that you would want to pursue. Right now, the amniotic fluid is packed full of genetic information about the baby. Amniotic fluid can be extracted for testing, but it doesn't need to be done for every pregnancy. This is ideal particularly when there is a family history of health conditions like sickle cell anemia, Downs Syndrome, or Tay-Sachs, among a variety of other disorders. It may also be recommended if other screening procedures have come back with abnormalities. If you have a relatively healthy family history and your screenings up to this point have all pointed to a healthy baby, amnio may not have to be on the table at all, but it's definitely worth the discussion. The plus side if you do decide to go for an amnio is that, with all that genetic information, they can determine the gender of the baby genetically, if you're really antsy to find out what you're having.

It's also time to decide if you want to pursue a birthing class. These classes often take about eight to twelve weeks to cover, so if it's on the priority list for you, it's time to start looking into classes near you. These classes will provide you with the knowledge and practical skills necessary to help you be a supportive partner to the best of your ability when the time comes, and for Mom to be prepared for what she's about to endure.

WEEK 16

How is Baby?

Baby's eyes and ears are beginning to function! Despite the eyelids still being fused shut, the baby can now shift its eyes back and forth, registering and responding to light sources. Within the baby's ears, the bones that help us to hear are settling into place and picking up on sound vibrations. The sounds are likely pretty muffled, but now the baby can pick up on the sounds of voices, music, and your pets if you have any.

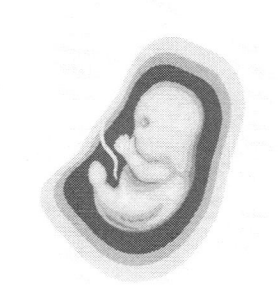

The baby is also preparing for some pretty major growth spurts. Over the coming weeks, baby will double in size from where they are now. Everything is growing at an incredible pace; their heart is pumping up to 25 quarts of blood every day, the tissues of lungs and other organs are developing, the kidneys, pancreas, liver, and other digestive organs have begun to function, and their hair and nails are really coming into their own.

How is Mom?

Now that Mom's belly is really starting to grow, she may be starting to feel itchy where the skin is expanding. Stretch marks aren't avoidable if she's genetically predisposed to them, but she can make them a little better by slathering on a really good hydrating lotion or oil. That expanding belly means she may need to go shopping for some new maternity wear, if she hasn't already. The belly growing also means that back pain is going to be on the rise. Instead of laying out on the couch, which will only provide temporary relief, doing things like stretching and prenatal yoga can be helpful in strengthening and stretching those muscles to provide some relief and support as the belly keeps growing.

Pregnancy hormones are also bringing some positives and negatives to the table right now. On one hand, Mom may be experiencing some itchy, dry eyes with a side of pregnancy brain, but on the other, the hormones are bringing on the pregnancy glow. Her skin is clearing up, and maybe she's having to do less with her skin routine to look and feel the best she has this entire pregnancy. As long as she's using pregnancy-safe products, she can keep that glow going.

How Can Dad Help?

Now that Mom's belly is growing pretty significantly, she's going to have to adjust how she sleeps. While you may love a good cuddle before going to sleep, she may need to get comfortable in new side positions. As her belly keeps growing, help her by positioning pillows around her; one under the belly can provide support and pain relief, as well as one behind the back and between her knees.

Since baby is starting to see and hear, now you can start joining Mom on the fun of experiencing the baby. If the baby has reached the point where you're able to feel the little kicks, you can start playing with the baby; if you lay your ear on Mom's belly, you can sometimes hear the baby's movements and tiny sounds, and if you direct a flashlight onto her belly, the baby may actually respond by moving away from the light. Talking to the baby is also a great way to bond, and get the baby used to your voice before they're even born. Doing things like reading them stories, telling baby about your day, or just generally chatting with Mom with your head by her belly are all nice ways to have those bonding moments before the baby is ever born.

WEEK 17

How is Baby?

Baby's heartbeat is double the rate of ours, about 140-150 beats a minute. The heartbeat is becoming more steady as their body becomes more regulated in the usage of its organs. As the organs become more regulated, the practice the baby has been getting has been slowly making it a champ at swallowing amniotic fluid and sucking its thumb. By the time the baby is born, eating and suckling will be second nature. This week, the baby's hearing is developing even more, so they'll better hear your voice or music you might play for them. They're also steadily putting on the baby fat that will keep them warm, not to mention squishy and cute, once they emerge into the world. Soon enough, their skin won't be so translucent. This is also the point when the baby really becomes their individual self, developing tiny fingerprints on their fingers and toes.

How is Mom?

While some of the strange pregnancy dreams may have begun in early pregnancy, they only get stranger as the hormones start to alter the brain. That's not the only sleep change she'll deal with though (this will mostly affect you); snoring. Get a humidifier into the room, and encourage Mom to sleep on her side so that you can catch some rest too.

Mom is really going to have to step up her stretching, to prevent and relieve sciatic pain. This nerve starts in the lower back, and runs downwards through the buttocks, legs, and ankles. As her belly grows and creates a deeper curve in her lower back, she may find that the sciatic nerve is pinched, so getting a warm compress on the area and following it up with prenatal back stretches can go a long way in relieving that pain.

This is also roughly the point that stretch marks start to appear over the belly, boobs, legs, and/or bum. Mom has been putting on weight fairly quickly, and some of the itchiness that she's experiencing is her skin trying to keep up with the rapid stretching of her skin. Lotions and moisturizing oils help to reduce the itchiness all over, and can help to prevent some of the additional stretch marks that come about.

How Can Dad Help?

Getting excited to meet the baby? Within the next few weeks, you should be seeing the gender in the ultrasound, usually between the 18 and 20-week scans. There's no better time to start talking about baby names, if you haven't chosen one already.

You may also have to become the tummy referee. Once Mom starts showing, people tend to think that it's no problem to reach over and start touching her belly. Especially when she's already itchy and sore among her other pregnancy symptoms, having someone constantly touching her belly without asking can't be the most pleasant. Be ready to subtly protect the belly if Mom is feeling uncomfortable; even if it's just getting your hand to her belly before the person can start touching, it can help enforce the boundary of "please don't touch Mom without permission."

WEEK 18

How is Baby?

Your baby is starting to take shape, and really look like the baby that will be born. Their ears have found their forever home on the sides of the baby's head, and even more exciting, the baby's sex organs are in place and fully formed. This means that on your next ultrasound appointment, you very well could be finding out the gender of your baby! When looking at the ultrasound, the baby might still be hiding that knowledge with the way they've positioned themselves, but a surefire way to know what you're having is really peering in on the shapes. A baby girl will have what looks like three lines on the ultrasound, whereas a baby boy will look familiar to Dad, as it's pretty clearly an external organ sticking up.

Not so obvious on an ultrasound is the baby's other major development this week: their developing nervous system. In order for impulses to be transferred through the nervous system, to our brain, and then back out to produce our reactions, our nerves need a coating of myelin, which is like a slick fat coating on the nerve pathways to help the messages travel as quickly as possible through the nervous system. This myelin coating is developing this week, so hopefully your baby will develop some lightning-fast reflexes some day.

Finally, baby has learned a new trick this week; when they're tired, they now yawn. You might even catch a peek at their tiny yawn in the ultrasound!

How is Mom?

For now, most of Mom's symptoms are more or less the same as they have been. Some swollen feet after a long day standing, sore back, maybe some congestion, and the other typical symptoms that she's been feeling up to this point. There are a couple new ones that might be presenting themselves around this time though; one, she may start feeling a little unsteady. Not dizzy, but off balance, since the growing baby is throwing off her center of gravity, making her a little more clumsy than usual. Two, she might be getting quite the appetite these days. Specific food cravings and an insatiable hunger that seem to want to consume absolutely everything in sight is pretty normal.

How Can Dad Help?

Getting in with a pediatrician can take a long time. This is the ideal time to find the pediatrician who will be looking after your little one after they arrive, since meeting doctors and waiting lists can take a while, depending on where you are. The pediatrician will likely be coming in to meet the baby within the first day or two of being born, so it's best to already have someone lined up sooner than later.

If Mom is struggling with the effects of relaxin, she may be due for a pregnancy massage. Relaxin is a hormone that does exactly what it sounds like; it relaxes the joints and ligaments to allow for Mom's body to expand for baby, and start repositioning for when the big day comes. If she's really sore and struggling, there are some prenatal massages that can be done in various spas and massage centers that accommodate for the growing belly, as well as restrictions on heat and types of oils not safe for a pregnant person.

Finally, it's also time to start considering maternity leave, and discussing when Mom will be putting in her paperwork to take leave. It's important to give her employer plenty of time to figure out staffing, and also to give your employer time as well if you'll be taking any amount of leave to help with the baby and Mom's recovery.

WEEK 19

How is Baby?

Baby is now in sensory overdrive. The nerves that were developing over the last week have now given the baby a stronger sense of taste, smell, hearing, touch, and sight, so they're experiencing the womb in a whole new way. Baby's lungs are also continuing their development, and will continue to do so until the final weeks of pregnancy, when they'll be mature enough to function on their own.

In new developments, baby is forming a new layer that will cover up their skin. You know how your fingers and toes look when you've been sitting in water for a long time? The new wax-like coating, called vernix caseosa, will cover up the baby's sensitive skin so that your baby doesn't exit the womb looking more like a prune than a baby. This waxy, almost cheese-like substance does start to come off towards the end of the pregnancy, but babies born early may still be sporting their waxy coat.

How is Mom?

Mom is most likely pretty achy right now. Leg cramps, back aches, and swelling in the feet, hands, and maybe even legs have become her norm these days, which isn't likely to be the most comfortable thing in the world. The plus side is that baby is moving on a regular basis now, and it's pretty amazing to experience. She's probably finding it pretty difficult to get comfortable, and unfortunately it's not going to get much better until the baby arrives. Pillows are about to become her best friend.

She's also going to have to be on the lookout for yeast infections. Unfortunately, pregnant women can be prone to them, and from this stage of the pregnancy and going forward, they're even harder to treat and get under control. If she's showing symptoms, it's time to talk to her medical provider for a pregnancy-safe option to resolve the infection before it gets out of control.

How Can Dad Help?

For now, just do what you can to help keep her comfortable, which is going to be pretty difficult to do at some points. If she's hungry, try to (gently!) make recommendations for healthy greens, fiber, and lots of water. If you were a kid that loved to build pillow forts when you were young, use those skills to help your pregnant partner find comfort if at all possible, and otherwise, just give her an ear to voice her excitement and concerns. If you have any skills in massage, a foot rub or back rub will also go a long way from here on out.

WEEK 20

How is Baby?

So far, baby is practicing their sucking and swallowing, and working towards perfecting their organs. They're also enjoying their new senses, and likely becoming much more active. Their organs are in place and functioning, so from here on out, they're going to be developing their organs and reflexes so that they're ready to use once the baby is out in the world.

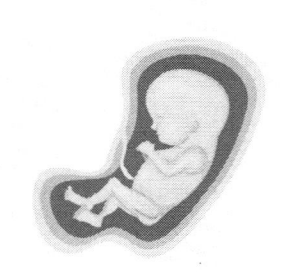

How is Mom?

Mom is officially halfway through her pregnancy, so she may be celebrating that she's completed half the journey. In a few weeks, she'll be reaching the third trimester, so that end stretch is probably looking really sweet to her right about now! You may have noticed something new about her belly this week; her 'innie' belly button may have 'popped' and is now an 'outie.' This is normal, and her belly button will return to normal after she delivers.

Otherwise, Mom is likely going through a rotation of feeling restless and exhausted, and spurts of high energy. Those energy levels will probably dip in the third trimester though, so if she has anything she wants to get done for the baby, it should probably get started up about now. Some of the fatigue may be coming from depleted iron levels, so if she hasn't been using an iron supplement, she may benefit from starting one now.

How Can Dad Help?

This is usually a good time to put together the baby registry if you and your partner haven't already, and time to talk about what is the preferred baby shower style for Mom. If you are planning to do it Jack and Jill style, or if you prefer to do them separately, it's time to discuss with each other first, and then family and friends can be called upon to get everything arranged.

If you haven't already talked about it, it may also be time to look into where Mom wants to give birth. It's important that Mom is comfortable when she's giving birth, so it's time to start figuring out the details and setting plans into motion so that she can get to where she wants to be once labor begins.

WEEK 21

How is Baby?

Baby is becoming far more coordinated these days, doing a lot more flexing, stretching, kicking, and even playing with the umbilical cord. Despite the fact that it may seem like the baby never stops moving, they're actually beginning to sleep as much as a newborn.

How is Mom?

Stretch marks, soreness, and restlessness aside, Mom might be feeling some anxiety right now. Feeling the baby kick is a wonderful feeling, but it may be setting in that this is really happening; in about 19 weeks, there's going to be a tiny life that you two will be taking care of.

Braxton-Hicks contractions may be starting soon. Think of them as practice contractions. They'll be irregular, and pretty inconsistent throughout the remainder of the pregnancy. They can definitely be alarming the first few times Mom experiences them, since they seem to come on out of nowhere, and they might gradually become stronger as she gets closer to delivery day.

Mom might need to get herself some nursing pads soon. Her breasts are deep in their preparations for nursing the baby, so Mom might experience some leaking in the coming weeks.

How Can Dad Help?

Keep on supporting as you have been for now. If you've started birth prep classes, use some of the breathing techniques that you're learning to help Mom get through the Braxton-Hicks contractions.

WEEK 22

How is Baby?

Baby's new favorite activity right now is grabbing at everything; their nose, their ears, and the umbilical cord. They're still developing their senses, and listening to Mom's heartbeat, digestion, and voice, as well as yours! They're becoming even more responsive to light, so feel free to play with them (as much as Mom has the patience for.) The baby's hair is also growing in right now, but there's no way to know just how much they'll have come their birthday.

How is Mom?

The hormones that were giving Mom her lush hair and long, strong nails are now working against her. The hair growth is now extending beyond her head, and probably growing thicker pretty much everywhere else. She'll have to be aware of how she typically removes hair if she chooses to; it's getting a lot harder for her to bend to shave, and some methods of hair removal, like lasers, bleach, and other chemicals are better to avoid during pregnancy. She may also experience her nails getting more brittle these days, and her once-glowing skin is now starting to break out, thanks to extra oil production. She may need to switch up her skin care products to reduce oil, and offer better moisturization.

How Can Dad Help?

Your focus going forward is going to center mostly on keeping Mom comfortable, and helping her to relax. Stay engaged with her needs, and help where you can. Pillows, healthy comfort foods, and a listening ear are going to be some of your best tools, along with foot and back rubs.

WEEK 23

How is Baby?

Baby's skin is starting to sag, almost like an ill-fitting suit. Luckily, their skin will be filling out soon, since the skin is developing faster than the baby fat. The skin may be developing a nice rosy hue as well, all thanks to the blood vessels that are developing just under the surface of the skin. While their skeleton and organs might be visible through their skin right now, the fat stores will fill in soon enough so Mom gives birth to a healthy, chubby cutie.

How is Mom?

For now, Mom's symptoms are likely at a plateau; she's not really developing any new symptoms, but they're not going away either. If she needs something fun to boost her spirits and help her feel better, she should consider a dance class; it's great for developing the support muscles that help her alleviate pain, keep her weight gain in its healthiest range, and is great for her mental health. A bonus is that the baby will be able to feel her dancing, and may move along with her!

How Can Dad Help?

Keep on helping in Mom's relaxation, and help her in tackling the issues that may be stressing her out. At some point, you may need childcare for when Mom goes back to work. Much like pediatricians, daycares and sitters may have long wait lists, so it's best to get onto finding one sooner than later.

WEEK 24

How is Baby?

At the moment, baby is looking very white. The hair from their head to their toes is completely without pigment right now, so it's all very white. Pigment will come in eventually, but for now, the color of baby's hair and eyes is up in the air. While the baby is waiting for that pigment, they're slowly packing on baby fat.

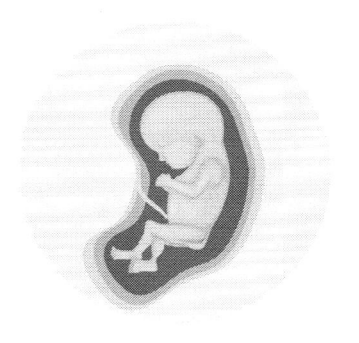

Now that the baby's hearing is getting better, play some music or sing for them! When a baby hears a song frequently in utero, they may associate it to being a comfort after they're born, so pick a song to sing or play that you feel will be a good comfort for the baby, and won't drive Mom and Dad up the wall right away.

How is Mom?

Pregnancy hormones strike again. In this case, it's coming in the form of numbness and pain through the wrists and hands; good ol' carpal tunnel syndrome. If Mom is experiencing carpal tunnel, getting good wrist braces—as well as avoiding sleeping on her hands and keeping them elevated when lying down to rest—will help. While typical carpal tunnel is associated with repetitive motion in the wrists, pregnancy carpal tunnel comes from fluids collecting in the extremities that are putting pressure on the nerves. Luckily, Mom isn't likely to need surgery for her carpal tunnel, as it usually goes away with giving birth.

Mom might also be struck with some odd symptoms like skin tags, or her palms and soles of her feet may become red and itchy. These are normal symptoms for this stage of pregnancy, but in rare cases it may be an indicator of a disorder called cholestasis of pregnancy. This is related to bile production within the gallbladder being slowed or stopped thanks to the pregnancy, but it's highly uncommon. If Mom is dealing with redness and itchiness, and tests negative for cholestasis of pregnancy, the only real cure for it is delivery, so she should avoid things that make it worse, like long hot showers or doing dishes without rubber gloves on. Sometimes a soak in cold water can provide some relief.

How Can Dad Help?

Mom's glucose screening is probably this week, where they'll check for gestational diabetes. Support her through the appointment, and otherwise focus on soothing her worries and discomfort. You're likely becoming quite the pro at that by this point. It can also help to educate yourself on the signs of preterm labor, just in case. It's better to be prepared with the knowledge and not need it, versus not having the knowledge and having no idea what is happening or what to do.

WEEK 25

How is Baby?

Baby's lungs will be developing through the rest of the pregnancy, but right now, they're using their nose more to figure out breathing. Of course, there's no air in the womb, but they're going to be breathing in amniotic fluid, as well as working on their sense of smell. This comes thanks to the amino acids, proteins, and other minerals imparted by Mom's food, so the baby will have an idea of what their parents eat on a regular basis. If baby is growing a good head of hair, you may be able to see the texture of the hair in the next ultrasound. Otherwise, baby is steadily putting on more weight in preparation for their big arrival.

How is Mom?

Swollen varicose veins and spider veins aren't uncommon in pregnancy. Unfortunately, this also applies to the veins within the rectum, resulting in hemorrhoids in roughly half of pregnant women. If this is the case for Mom, she should focus on getting both fiber and extra water. If constipation is plaguing her, she should get a short stool to put her feet on while on the toilet, to help move things along a little easier.

Round ligament pain may be coming and going for some, as well as a condition called symphysis pubis dysfunction. The hormone relaxin is to blame for this one, since it's relaxing the ligaments and joints throughout the pelvis. An exercise ball and working on the pelvic floor muscles can help relieve the worst of the symptoms of symphysis pubis dysfunction.

Hormones can also be affecting her eyesight right now. If she's always had perfect vision, she might find herself squinting to see things that she never would have had issue with before. While the change in eyesight can sometimes be permanent, it typically returns to normal after having the baby.

Finally, if anxiety and depression are ramping up right now, Mom should consider speaking to her doctor about it. The stress of pregnancy symptoms making her feel crappy, topped with worries of the future, plus the compounding hormones can really be getting to Mom right now. She should be speaking to her doctor or therapist, as well as her support system of family and friends to help reduce the stress, and hopefully have a happier pregnancy.

How Can Dad Help?

This is preparation time! If you've found a pediatrician, start talking to them about recommendations of what to buy and not buy for baby. You may also want to start rearranging your kitchen to make meal prep a little easier and quicker, and start getting used to meals that offer nutrition, while also being quick and easy to make while minimizing clean up. When baby arrives, both you and Mom likely won't be too interested in cooking major meals, so start figuring out meals now that will be easily made when you're both sleep deprived and lacking in energy.

WEEK 26

How is Baby?

Those little eyes that have been fused shut for months are finally starting to open! They're complete with lovely eyelashes as baby checks out their environment that they've been floating around in for the last two trimesters.

Baby's brain activity is also bumping up this week, so they're starting to actually react, compared to their earlier responses coming from nerves firing off during brain development. Their startle reflex is coming in, among other reflexes, that will help the baby to figure out the world when they arrive.

How is Mom?

Heartburn, restless leg syndrome, cramping, back aches, and a squirming baby are probably making it impossible for Mom to sleep these days. Insomnia normally sets in right about now, but luckily, Mom is going into the home stretch. Clumsiness, migraines, and pregnancy brain are likely all on the rise, thanks to the hormones and lack of sleep. Mom is probably feeling like she should just move into the bathroom by now, with a karate-kicking baby pummeling her bladder. Only 14 weeks left before she starts feeling more like herself!

SECOND TRIMESTER 105

How Can Dad Help?

If gifts are starting to roll in from family and friends, it's time to start going through them to make sure that they'll be safe for the baby. Especially secondhand items should be checked over thoroughly to make sure they're meeting today's safety requirements. If the items are deemed safe and secure for your baby, it's a great time to get everything set up in the baby's nursery. You can also go through the house and consider what will need to be babyproofed and moved around.

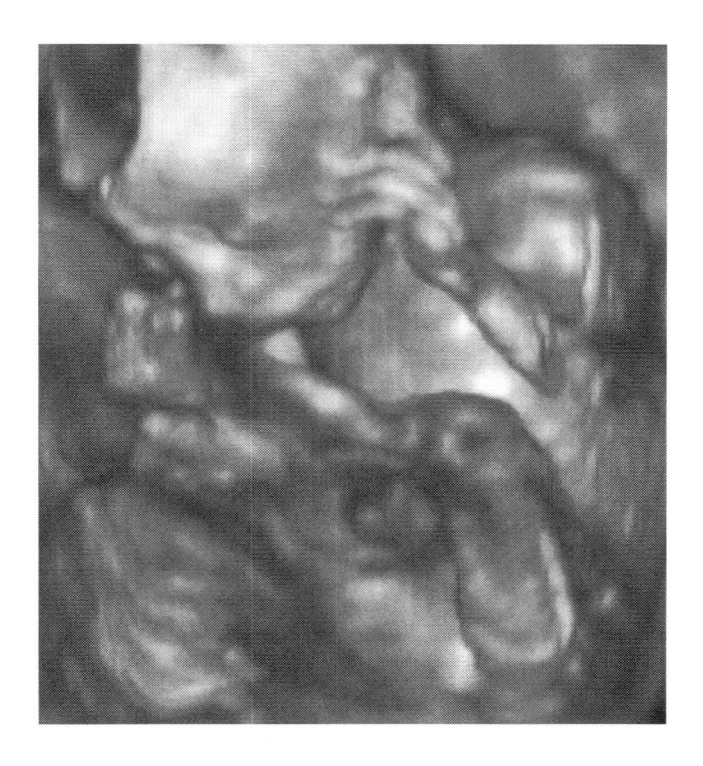

CHAPTER 7
THIRD TRIMESTER

> "Life is a flame that is always burning itself out, but it catches fire again every time a child is born." — George Bernard Shaw

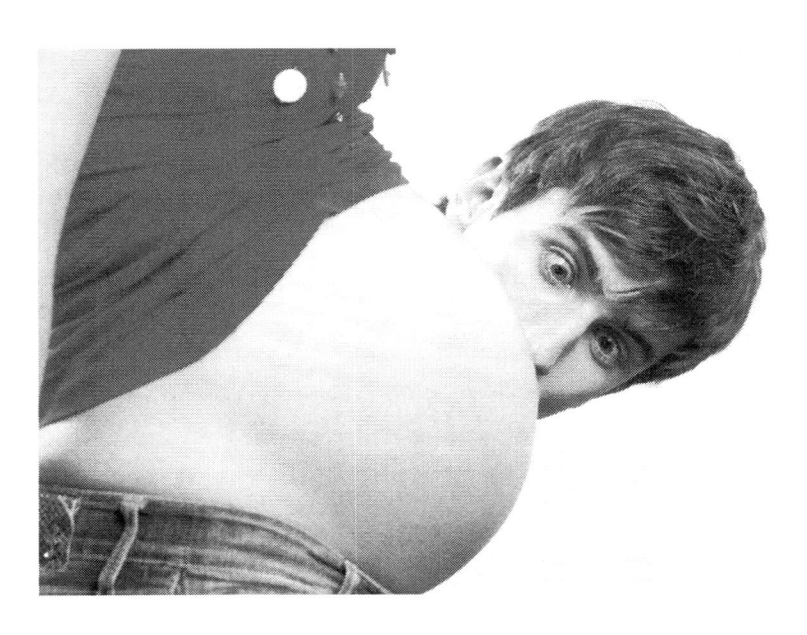

WELCOME to the final stretch of pregnancy! 13 short weeks from now, you'll likely be holding your baby, and setting off on your new lifestyle. Baby is going to finish up with their development this trimester, and Mom is likely to get a lot more uncomfortable this trimester. You may see a resurgence of first trimester symptoms, as well as some new ones that come with fluctuating hormone levels and the expansion of Mom's belly. This whole trimester will likely be spent scrutinizing every symptom for signs of labor. Updates get shorter this month as Mom's symptoms get more consistent, and baby finishes cooking up in Mom's oven.

WEEK 27

How is Baby?

As the baby grows, you might feel some small, odd movements from the baby; as the baby's diaphragm and lungs develop, they start to get the hiccups! They can even get hiccups if Mom has been enjoying spicy meals, since they're not accustomed to those types of foods yet.

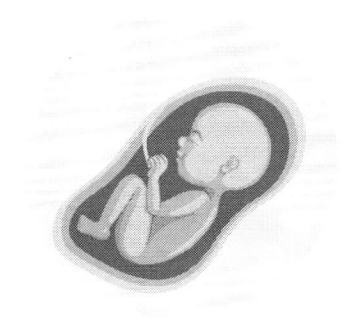

The baby is also reaching a point where they may recognize and respond to the sound of voices they hear regularly. Granted, the sound is muffled through their waxy vernix coat and the layers of muscle and tissue of Mom's belly, but by the time they're born, they'll be fully familiar with you and Mom's voice.

How is Mom?

This trimester, Mom should be expecting sweat. Between carrying the extra weight of the baby and the mix of hormones at play, she should be staying hydrated, and doing what she can to wick the extra sweat away. With this comes swelling extremities and potentially heat rash. She might also notice that her belly itches even more as it continues to expand; keep moisturizing lotions and oils handy to help relieve the itch without scratching. Here's a little tip for Mom: if you *must* scratch, use your knuckles!

Now that baby is getting a lot bigger, Mom might be finding it hard to keep control of her bladder. Laughing and sneezing are going to be risky if she doesn't want to pee herself, especially if she's staying on top of hydrating properly.

How Can Dad Help?

Two areas you can help right now is researching car seats, and getting into an infant CPR course. The safety standards for car seats are updated regularly by manufacturers and governments, so make sure the one you choose is the safest option for your baby and your vehicle. As for CPR; let's be honest, babies aren't great at swallowing in the beginning, and they love putting things into their mouths. Knowing how to handle a choking baby is invaluable in those life-threatening situations.

This is also a great time to be talking to family and friends about making sure their vaccines are up to date. Whooping cough vaccines, for example, don't cover a person for their entire lives, and whooping cough can be lethal for an infant. Anyone who is coming in to visit the baby, especially as a newborn, should make sure they're vaccinated, wash their hands, and don't kiss the baby for any reason. All kinds of viruses can be passed from a kiss to a baby, so play it safe while their immune system develops.

WEEK 28

How is Baby?

By now, baby is settling into their final birthing position. Their development is progressing; they are sticking out their tongue, blinking their eyes now that the lids are no longer fused, and even dreaming! At this point, the baby can experience REM sleep, which is the point in our sleep where we dream, so they may be dreaming about meeting you and Mom!

How is Mom?

Now that Mom is in the home stretch, she will be getting even more uncomfortable. Sciatic and lower back pain are on the rise, and in combination with the heat rash and sweating she may be experiencing, she may find that her skin is becoming even more sensitive lately. Breathable fabrics, SPF, and lots of water will help to decrease her discomfort.

How Can Dad Help?

If you've chosen a location to birth, it may be a good idea to go down for a tour and get a rundown of what birthing in that location may look like. Reaching the delivery room is going to be a different experience for every couple and every pregnancy, so you're better off knowing where you need to go and what is available to you and Mom, instead of panicking when you arrive.

It's also time to have the circumcision talk if you're having a boy. Some places will no longer automatically provide circumcisions, but if it is a part of your religious or cultural practice, it should be discussed soon.

This is also the point to start counting kicks! There are a variety of apps to choose from to make it easier, and it'll give you an idea of your baby's activity. Try to count at the same time every day, preferably at a time when the baby is usually active. That way, if there's ever any concern about the baby's activity, you have a baseline for activity that you can reference back to and know what is normal for the baby.

WEEK 29

How is Baby?

Baby is focusing on putting on fat, so their wrinkly suit-like skin is filling out with more squish. They may even begin smiling this week, particularly while dreaming. With the baby putting on weight and the womb getting much tighter, their kicks and movements are going to be more prominent, and may be more like a jab than a kick.

How is Mom?

Restless leg syndrome usually sets in for a lot of moms during the third trimester. If Mom can keep moving about, it may help to reduce the effects, and let her get some of the rest she desperately needs. Braxton-Hicks contractions can also happen more often, so having a contraction counter can help to recognize when the true contractions have started.

How Can Dad Help?

How is the nursery coming along? Mom is getting more uncomfortable, so getting the nursery decorated and filled in will take a good amount off your plate, in terms of planning for baby's arrival.

If you and Mom have been interested in banking cord blood, now is the time to ask your doctor about the process. Cord blood can be an incredible resource, and more parents are considering the painless procedure: whether to have it banked or donated. Discuss with Mom if it's something that you may want to have done.

WEEK 30

How is Baby?

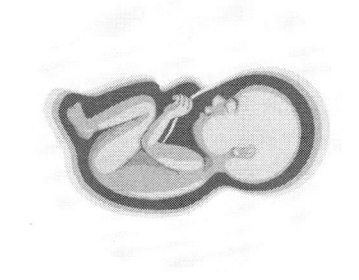

Baby is putting all of their energy into developing their brain right now. Little wrinkles are developing over the surface of their brain, making room for new brain cells. They're also developing their grip strength, so in future ultrasounds, you may see the baby grabbing their feet or playing with the umbilical cord, which serves as their only toy in the womb. Now that the baby is putting on fat, the lanugo is starting to shed, so baby likely won't be super furry on their way out into the world.

How is Mom?

Some of the less comfortable pregnancy symptoms of the first trimester may be making a return at this point. The biggest one is typically heartburn; that baby has strong legs, and they're probably pushing on the stomach pretty firmly. Mom is most likely experiencing fatigue all over again, combined with an aching body, and potentially even returned morning sickness.

How Can Dad Help?

Pillows are probably going to be Mom's best friend. Do what you can to keep Mom comfortable, because the next ten weeks aren't going to be super comfortable. If Mom usually likes heels, it may be time to keep some flats in the car for her, just in case the swelling gets to be too much. Speaking of the car, try doing a test drive from your work or home to the hospital, so you know exactly how much time you're working with when labor starts. Remember to add in time for traffic depending what time of day you'll be going.

WEEK 31

How is Baby?

Baby's brain is in overdrive, making new connections within the brain to develop the five senses. They'll be sleeping a lot more while their brain develops, and moving a lot more than before when they're awake.

How is Mom?

You can expect a lot of the same in the coming weeks; Mom is short of breath, her back constantly hurts, and pregnancy brain has her looking for the glasses that are sitting on her head.

How Can Dad Help?

It's time to get the hospital bag locked and loaded with everything you need, since you never know when labor might start. Start packing the things you'll need as you think about them, and refer to Chapter 8 to get a better idea of things you might need to pick up.

Now that Mom is getting much bigger around the belly, you might be wondering if it's still okay to have sex if she's in the mood. As long as her water isn't broken, she's safe to have sex if she wants to. There are no concerns over whether you might hurt the baby; in some cases, you may even lull the baby to sleep with the rocking motion.

WEEK 32

How is Baby?

With the exception of its lungs, your baby's organs are fully developed. If they were to be born now, they'd be viable, though would still need a little help breathing. They're already breathing in amniotic fluid, but their lungs aren't quite there yet.

How is Mom?

If Mom's breasts weren't leaking colostrum before, it may begin to happen soon. This means breast pads are going to help her stay dry, without the giant wet spots down the front of her shirt. Otherwise, her symptoms are likely staying consistent.

How Can Dad Help?

Get brushed up on the early labor signs, and be ready! At some point in the next two months you'll need the knowledge to recognize early labor if Mom doesn't pick up on it first.

WEEKS 33 - 40+

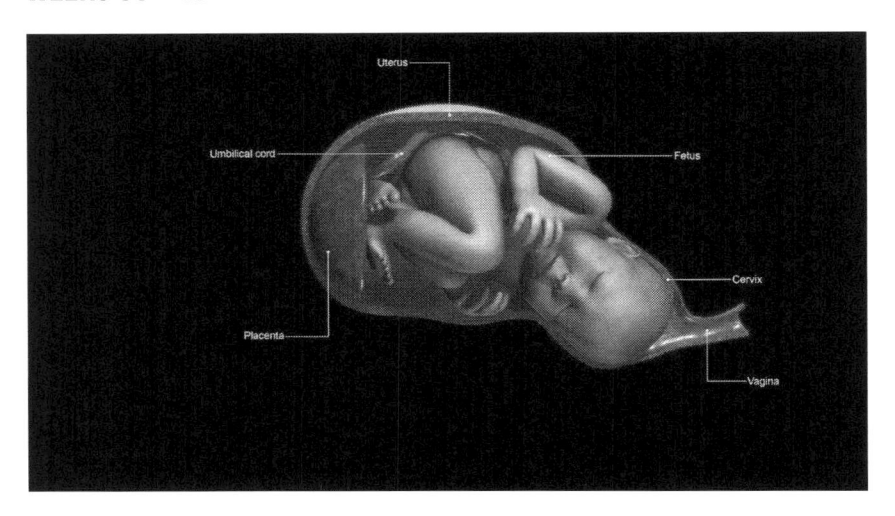

How is Baby?

Baby is making strides, and doing any fine tuning it needs. The baby fat has made it so that baby isn't so transparent, and the thinning uterus around them is letting them learn day from night. Their wax coating sloughs off during this period as well, leaving soft baby skin when they're born. More importantly, baby's immune system is finally developed! It's still new, but will continue its development over the next several years. From here on out, baby's development is solely focused on finishing up those lungs and the digestive system, and putting on baby fat.

How is Mom?

Insomnia, heartburn, and back pain are Mom's reality right now. Her bladder is going to be in overdrive for the rest of the pregnancy, and she's probably anxious for the baby's eviction date from her uterus. Braxton-Hicks contractions are probably giving her a run for her money, but before you know it, it'll be the real deal! She may also notice some vision changes again, with slight blurring. Her eyes should return to normal after delivery, but for now, she might need reading glasses.

How Can Dad Help?

This is the point where all the final details are put into place; getting the car seat secured in the car, making sure that the go-bag is ready, and double-checking everything in the nursery and house for babyproofing and safety. Get familiar with the baby gear you'll be using, so you're not figuring it out with a baby in your arms.

CHAPTER 8
GETTING READY FOR BIRTH

> "A new baby is like the beginning of all things – wonder, hope, a dream of possibilities." — Eda LeShan

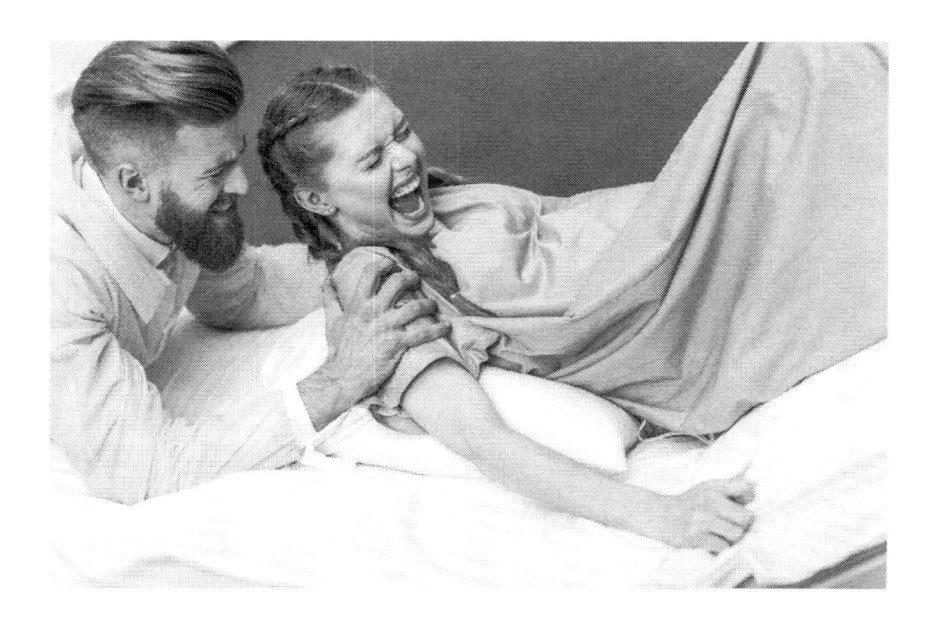

WHEN YOU'RE in the final weeks and months before the baby arrives, it's time to go over the final checklists to make sure that everything is ready for the magic moment when the baby decides to make their grand entrance into the world. Everything from getting the baby's areas in the house set up, making sure that all of the essentials are in place, having your hospital go-bag ready, and having one final big outing with your partner before the baby arrives are likely on your mind by this stage. The baby will be here soon! Are you ready?

ESSENTIALS FOR BABY'S ARRIVAL

If this is the first child between the two of you, figuring out what really is essential and what is a money-grab can be overwhelming. The best thing you can do is to talk to people who have recently had children; someone who had a baby ten plus years ago isn't going to be as keyed in to what is being used today, although they absolutely will have good advice along the way. As someone with multiple children in the last handful of years, this is what I'd recommend as the absolute essentials for your baby, especially in the first year:

- Lots of clothing in a variety of sizes. You won't need an extensive amount of the newborn size unless they're born a premie, or the baby is just very small when they're born. Most babies will grow out of a newborn size very quickly, so focus on having more in the 3-6 month and the 6-9 month sizes. On that note, it's often better to get infant clothing secondhand at consignment and other secondhand marketplaces. They'll grow out of the onesies and outfits you get them in a heartbeat, so save the brand-new purchases for the things that you know you're going to want to keep as a memento, like the first outfit they wore in the hospital, or the outfit you bring them home in. It's a good idea to have a decent amount of clothing for them though, as they'll often go through 2-6 outfits in a day just from spitting up and diaper blowouts alone. Be prepared to do a lot of laundry! I also recommend that if you're getting full body onesies, try to stick with the ones that have a zipper, rather than a whole bunch of buttons. The buttons are cute, but babies are squirmy, and some get sick of getting dressed pretty quickly. If it's a onesie that just has the three buttons in the diaper area, it's not so bad, as it can be done up quickly.

- On the note of clothing, don't get 20 pairs of shoes for an infant. For one, they can't walk. Second, they don't keep them on. It doesn't hurt to have a pair of booties in a few sizes for transporting them outdoors, especially in the winter months, but getting them shoes to go with every outfit is going to turn into a waste of money very, very quickly.
- Baby grooming sets. The nice thing is, most hospitals will provide things like aspirators, combs, and baby-appropriate nail clippers. Otherwise, keep it simple. You can usually find these kits at your local dollar store. Make sure that any shampoos or soaps that you use are free of strong scents and harsh chemicals for their sensitive skin.

- A variety of bibs. They make them with teethers on them, with scoops to catch food in when baby starts on solids, and in large and small sizes depending on absorbency needs. Once the baby starts teething, it's going to be drool city, so you're going to be changing the bibs quite often.
- Stockpile diapers. Newborn sizes—you can usually get away with only needing one, maybe two packs before they move on to the next size up, but the size one to three, you can't go wrong with having a good pile ahead of time. Newborn diapers are easier to pick up on an as-needed basis, versus having to find a way to get rid of several packages that you now don't need. This applies to cloth diapers as well, if you choose to go that route.
- Sample sizes of diaper creams. There are a few zinc-based diaper creams that some people swear by, but it really does depend on the baby. Test them out for your preference and what works best on your baby's skin, *then* go get the big container of the one that works.
- A diaper genie. You don't necessarily need to go for a specific brand, but definitely get a container that seals well for diapers if you're going the disposable diaper route. Even if you're going for cloth diapers and wipes, you'll want something that will seal so that the room, and by extension your house, doesn't smell like baby poop and urine constantly. If you're a family that changes the trash daily, dropping any solid waste into the toilet to be flushed, then rolling the diaper up to be tossed in your trash can should also be fine.

- Changing pad. This is a large foam pad with lifted edges and a strap to buckle in your squirmy baby. These are light and portable, so you can keep it where you spend the most time with your baby—and with the waterproof cover on it, you can keep your furniture safe from baby's waste.
- Some toys… but don't go too crazy. More often than not, if people aren't sure what they want to buy for your baby, they'll default to stuffed animals. Try not to go overboard on buying massive amounts of stuffed toys, and instead use the baby toy money on sensory objects, and toys that will help your baby when teething and figuring out how to use their hands. Keep it simple; after all, the baby is going to be in the "just trying to figure out how to be human" stage for a while, so a room packed with toys isn't going to make a difference to them for a while. Small things that fit in their hands but not in their mouths are great, especially if they make little noises and have different textures to experiment with.
- Moses basket. This is going to be a better alternative to a bassinet. It's small, and will make for a safe place for baby to sleep wherever you want them. Even if you put them down in the living room, but want them to sleep in their bedroom, they can be easily transported to the nursery, and the basket placed in the crib. Bassinets aren't used for very long, since they can only be used up to a certain size and weight, so you're better off with a Moses basket and crib combo.

- Crib. On that note, definitely get yourself a crib sooner than later. It's better to get them used to the crib right away, so find something that will fit into your room while the baby shares the room, and that can be comfortably moved into the nursery when it comes time. If a crib won't fit comfortably in your room, a Pack N' Play is a great alternative, since many come with a lifted piece so that you can more comfortably bend to place and pick up baby.
- Baby monitors. There is a lot of variety on the market, but you don't necessarily have to go for the baby-branded monitors. There are lots of cheaper video and sound monitors that can connect to your phone that you can make sure are on a secure connection. These cameras can typically pick up sound and movement, and lots of them even have sensors to detect a person or a certain sound range so that you can hear the baby cry no matter where you are in the house.
- Baby feeding chair. While high chairs are the norm—and the baby absolutely needs a place to eat—high chairs can be a nightmare for storage and space, and have all kinds of nooks that food can get stuck in. Instead, a seat that attaches to the chairs of your dining set tends to be a lot better overall; they're usually more cost effective, easier to clean, they fit into the average dining room much easier, and they get your baby used to eating at the kitchen table right from the start.
- A stroller that suits your lifestyle. If you know that you're not someone who is a runner or jogger, an

expensive jogging stroller likely isn't for you. Choose something that you know will easily come together and collapse when needed, and matches the lifestyle you have.

- A car seat. In the beginning, most car seats are smaller carriers that can be clipped into a base. From there, you'll need something that fits into your car, and has the adjustments for angle and height as your baby grows. Pay attention to things like age conversion seats that will move from rear facing, to forward facing, to booster seat. Also avoid picking up a second-hand car seat from a source you don't know; if a car seat has been in an accident, there may be damaged components that can be dangerous if you were to be in an accident with your infant.

Nice to have but not essential:

- Wipe warmers. While they may seem like a nice luxury to keep your baby warm and comfortable, they can also be a breeding ground for bacteria. Holding the wipe in your hand for a few moments is often enough to warm it up, without risking an infection or rash for your little one.
- Changing table. While they may seem to be the ultimate necessity, the reality is that you're likely going to change your baby wherever it's convenient. It's not so bad if

you get a crib that ages with the baby into a toddler bed; some of those types do have an attached changing table that later becomes a part of the child's dresser. Going out and buying a changing table—especially if you know the baby's nursery is upstairs while you spend most of your time downstairs—ends up being a waste of money for many people. A changing pad that can be put down is a far better option if you're looking to save money.

- Bath thermometer. While the marketing for these little gadgets focuses on how sensitive baby's skin is—and of course we want to keep our baby from being burned—we can easily test the temperature with our hands. Lukewarm water is best, so save the money and just use your hands.
- Special "babies only" detergent. While there are plenty that are marketed specifically for babies, along with the "babies only" hefty price tag, what you really need to focus on is making sure that you're getting a detergent that is free of dyes, scents, and other additives. Plenty of all-natural laundry detergents cater to this while offering the cleaning power necessary for the mountains of laundry you're looking at.
- Excessive crib accessories. We love scrolling Instagram and seeing all of the perfectly matched aesthetic crib setups, with the bumpers and stuffed animals and pillows and matching blankets. While this is so cute to look at, it actually creates a hazard to your baby. Minimize what is in the crib so that you can minimize SIDS risk, and keep your baby safe. As the baby grows, having too many items in the crib also provides your

child with a means to climb out of their crib, and may result in injury if they fall.
- Baby tubs. There are plenty of seats on the market that make it easy for baby to be bathed in the sink or tub, and enjoying a bath or shower with your baby is one of the purest bonding moments you can have.
- "Baby Bullet" food processors. If you already have a food processor, it's going to do the exact same thing. There's nothing wrong with choosing to make your own baby food, but you don't need the baby branding that's going to raise the price for something half the size that'll clutter up your counter even more.
- A diaper bag. Even if you don't get one of the traditional branded diaper bags, choosing a favorite tote or backpack is going to do the job. As long as you have the room for the essentials that you'll need, like bottles, snacks, diapers, wipes, creams, and extra clothes in case of a mess.

HOSPITAL GO-BAG ESSENTIALS

Having a bag ready is key in making sure that nothing essential gets left behind in the rush to get to the hospital. There's never a real way to know that Mom is about to go into labor, unless you have a scheduled induction or c-section. If you don't have one of these scheduled appointments, get your hospital go-bag ready a few weeks in advance, just in case of an early labor. Things that will be necessary or helpful to keep in the go-bag include:

- Important documents. Anything that you may need, whether it's medical insurance, hospital forms that are pre-filled, or identification should be quickly accessible.
- Birth plan. Your birth plan should be kept with your hospital documents so that it is readily accessible to medical professionals. You never know if your usual doctor will be on rotation that night, so make sure that the information is thorough on the birth plan, on the off-chance that it's a new-to-you doctor delivering your baby.
- Cash. Keep a little bit of cash for vending machines or for use in the hospital cafeteria. It's always a 50/50 chance that the cafeteria in the hospital might use machines, or might be cash only, so better safe than sorry.
- Lip balm. Hospitals are very dry, so keep some lip balm or a chapstick on hand.
- Sugar-free hard candies or lozenges. Keep these sugar-free, since sugary candies can actually make Mom more thirsty. During active labor, Mom's water intake will be limited. This is for multiple reasons; if mom gets an epidural, getting up to go to the bathroom won't be possible, and when it comes time to start pushing, access to the urethra to empty the bladder may be difficult. While mom may be able to have a catheter for a while, depending on how labor is moving, if they have to regularly remove and reinsert the catheter, there is a chance for infection. If there is any reason that Mom may need to be put under for emergency surgery, keeping the stomach empty of fluids or food also

prevents the accidental aspiration of the contents of the stomach into the lungs. The final reason, of course, is it makes a doctor's job more difficult to do when they're dodging a stream of urine to the face.
- Headbands or hair ties. If Mom has long hair, it will help her to tie it back when active labor comes along. Labor can be a sweaty time, so Mom needs to be able to focus on what she's doing, rather than fussing with her hair being stuck to her eyelid or in her mouth.
- Toiletries. Don't forget things like deodorant, toothbrushes, toothpaste, hair brushes, and moisturizers. After the delivery, Mom will also at some point want to take a shower while still in the hospital, so make sure that she has shampoo, conditioner, and soap available to her.
- Towel. At least one good towel will likely be far more comfortable than the hospital towels available. They tend to be thin, small, and scratchy, so one of Mom's favorite towels will go a long way.
- Robe. Between making it more comfortable to walk to and from the shower, as well as being more comfortable to sit and breastfeed in (if Mom is planning on breastfeeding), a good, comfortable robe will make all the difference.
- Pillows. Much like hospital towels, hospital pillows don't tend to be the most luxurious on the planet. You'll likely spend a few days in the hospital, so make sure that everyone has every little bit of comfort available.
- Sweaters and other comfortable clothing. This is for both Mom and Dad. Hospital temperatures can be

unpredictable, so you'll want something that will keep you warm and comfortable, as well as something that gives you the option of keeping cool. Bring something that can easily be opened for Mom, such as a button up flannel or a zip up hoodie; something that will make it easiest for her to be checked over by doctors, or to feed the baby when needed. You should have a few changes of clothing for yourself, Mom, and the baby.

- Nursing pads and maternity bras. Regardless of whether or not Mom plans to breastfeed, nursing pads will help to alleviate the leaking, and the maternity bras will offer support when her breasts engorge with milk following the birth.
- Bottles. If you plan to bottle feed rather than breastfeed, it can be best to bring the bottles that you hope to use so that the baby gets acclimated to them right away. The hospital will have some bottles, and will often have samples of formula for you to choose from, but if you already have formula, it doesn't hurt to bring some along with you so the baby is on a consistent formula.
- Charging cord, laptop, and/or bluetooth speakers. At some point during the stay, you and Mom are going to want some kind of entertainment. Any cords should be extra long, since you never know where you'll find an outlet in the hospital room. The bluetooth speaker will also be helpful if Mom wants soothing music during labor. Having a nice long playlist pre-made can be helpful, since you never know how long labor is going to last. Headphones also don't hurt to have for when

Mom is up late breastfeeding, and wants to catch up on her shows in peace.
- Non-perishable snacks and water bottles. This is both for Dad to sustain himself with during labor, as well as for Mom to snack on between meals. Recovery and breastfeeding takes a lot of energy!
- Adult diapers. While the hospital will supply giant pads and mesh underwear to hold the pad in place, adult diapers tend to offer more comfort and peace of mind that everything will stay in place. Mom is going to be bleeding for a while, so she should be able to stay as comfortable as possible.

SIGNS OF LABOR

The body preparing to go into labor isn't as simple as tv and movies would have you believe; the water breaking and sending Mom into having contractions isn't actually typical. The signs of labor can actually start weeks ahead of the actual birth, so knowing what to look for can help when Mom is shouting at her belly "Will you come out already?!"

- *The baby drops.* Just when you think Mom's belly can't get any bigger or more pronounced, the baby decides to settle in. The baby shifts lower into Mom's pelvis, getting its head in position above the cervix and into the pelvic bone.
- *Joints start feeling more loose or sore.* The hormone production in Mom's body is shifting towards relaxing the body so that the baby can more easily make its way

out of the body. This means that the joints through her body are going to feel sore and loose, especially in the hips, knees, and ankles.

- *Cramping and pain through the lower back.* Mom's muscles are now shifting to get her body into the best position to birth in, which means she'll be feeling some soreness. The cramping might feel similar to menstrual cramps as her spine and hips begin to get into a slightly different position to accommodate the baby's arrival.
- *Bloody show.* This sounds way more graphic than it actually is. The bloody show comes along with losing the mucus plug—the mucus film that covers the cervix to protect the baby from infection—which begins to separate. This might happen in one big clump, or it might break down into smaller pieces that are hardly visible. In the days before labor begins, the vaginal discharge may become thicker and more pink in appearance.
- *Dilating cervix.* This can begin far before labor is impending; some women spend weeks or even months dilated to 1-3 centimeters. The cervix begins to dilate, opening to allow the baby to find its way into the world. Once labor really begins, the cervix will dilate up to 10 centimeters, allowing the baby to pass through the birth canal.
- *The water breaks.* This is one of the most commonly known signs of labor. This is a natural part of the process, caused by the baby's head putting pressure on the amniotic sac, causing it to rupture. When this happens, Mom might feel a little 'pop' feeling, followed

by a trickling of fluid, or sometimes a small gush. It may be helpful to put a pad in place so that the fluid can be collected, and Mom can track her fluid loss. If she's filling many pads in the span of a few hours, labor is definitely incoming!

- **Contractions.** The other best known indication of labor is the arrival of strong, steady contractions. While Mom has likely been experiencing Braxton-Hicks contractions for a while now—which are irregular in timing and can vary in intensity—true labor contractions will often be stronger. The contractions that set in before labor will be evenly spaced, getting closer together as the time for delivery gets nearer. While the intensity of Braxton-Hicks contractions will vary over time, labor contractions will gradually get stronger and more intense.

THE BIRTH

Expectations for the birth will differ depending on a variety of circumstances. A hospital birth will be a vastly different experience than a birthing center or home birth, and the care provider will also have a big influence on how the birth will proceed. Any health conditions that Mom had prior to the pregnancy, or that she developed during pregnancy, will also alter the expectations that you might have for the birth. When it comes to what to expect, it is best to consult with your medical care provider to cover anything that may occur, as it can be detrimental to Mom's birthing and postpartum recovery to go in with ideas of what the birth will look like without the realistic approach of the person who will be guiding the birthing procedure. Every pregnancy and delivery will likely look different, so expectations should stay open and fluid. Much like the birth plan, the birthing experience is unpredictable, so be ready to go with the flow of progress, and know that unexpected changes may occur, if necessary to the health and wellness of mother and child.

What Can Dad Do?

When it comes time for the birth, the best thing that you can do is be there for support, and be an active partner for Mom to rely on. Taking a Lamaze or Bradley Method class can help you to be an active participant in the birth. These classes will provide knowledge on breathing techniques, wellness during pregnancy, and hands-on practice with pain relief techniques. If these classes are not available to you, or if they weren't within your budget, learn about helping Mom to breathe through the pain, and be there as a support to hold her hand, wipe away sweat to keep it out of her eyes, and otherwise help Mom and the birthing care professional with anything they may require assistance with. Learning techniques to apply pressure on the hips and back to relieve the pain can go a long way.

CHAPTER 9
THE FOURTH TRIMESTER

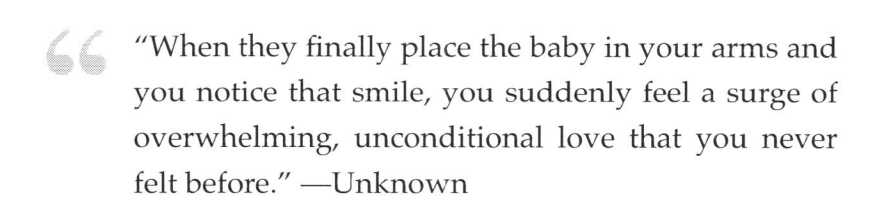

> "When they finally place the baby in your arms and you notice that smile, you suddenly feel a surge of overwhelming, unconditional love that you never felt before." —Unknown

THE NEXT PERIOD following the birth of your child is known to many prenatal and postnatal professionals as the "fourth trimester." This window of time is for Mom's recovery and adjustment to now being a mother. This includes you, too. How you support her is going to make a big difference to how she perceives *her* world, especially while looking through hormone goggles.

FINDING YOUR ROUTINE

Your entire world is going to revolve around this new baby, as well as taking care of Mom, who is also entirely focused on the baby. I guarantee, there has never been a point in your life where you've been so obsessed with another person's bathroom habits as when you are the one changing diapers and literally watching their digestive system mature by looking at the contents.

It's important that both you and Mom alternate on having time on your own, as well as finding moments for yourselves to still feel like a couple. Little routines like watching a movie, cooking together, or making each other coffee shouldn't go down the drain; this time period is about nurturing bonds. Bonds with each other, bonds with baby, and bonds with your mental health. The window may only be five minutes, but five minutes to stare out a window with a hot coffee can make the difference, if you take the opportunity.

Feeding Times

Baby is going to be pretty much constantly eating in the first weeks; roughly every two to three hours, depending on their appetite. If Mom is breastfeeding, you can offer support by burping baby and bringing her water and snacks, as breastfeeding does take a lot out of her. If bottle feeding, alternate on feedings.

Sleep

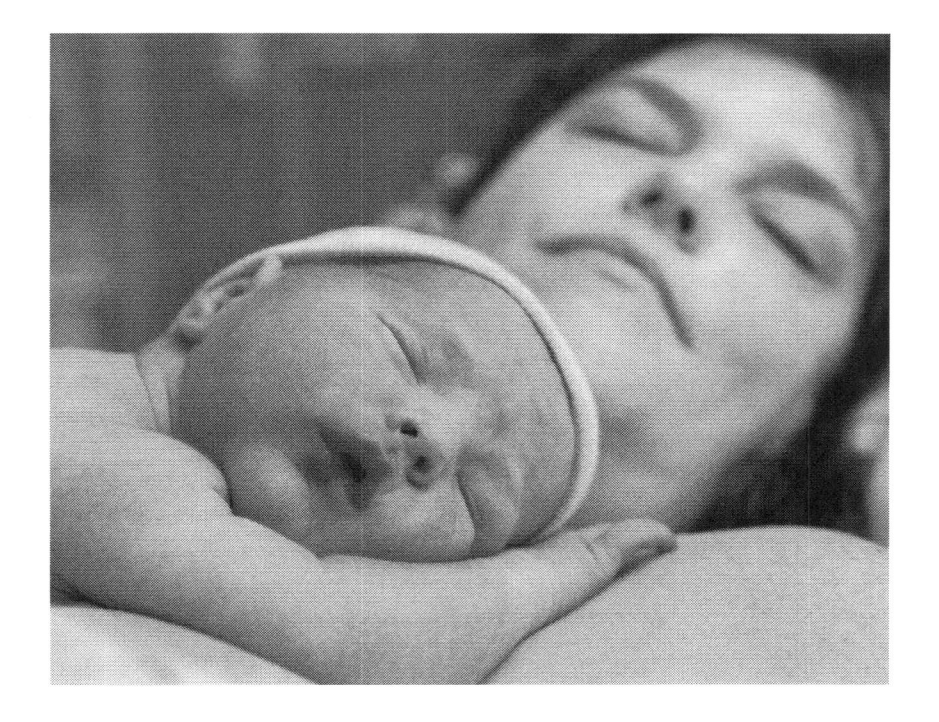

"Sleep when the baby sleeps" is such a load of diaper filler for most families. It's probably some of the most common advice that you'll get as new parents, and for most people, it simply doesn't work that way. Why? Because when baby sleeps, you finally have the time to do the things you need to catch up on, like cleaning bottles, and doing the mountain of laundry this tiny human has somehow managed to create in the span of a day, or cleaning the breast pump, or just taking time to breathe *alone*. You might even catch yourself staring at this tiny creature you and your partner created, and what feels like minutes suddenly becomes a half hour. Before you know it, the baby shrieks awake, and you realize you've missed out on your *you* time until the next nap. If you're lucky, you might catch a nap when the baby is napping, but otherwise, it almost always seems to be that when you finally lay down and decide to try to catch a little bit of shut eye, the baby pops awake demanding comfort, attention, and maybe a diaper change.

Nighttime Wake-ups

For the first weeks, months, and sometimes even years, don't expect to be getting your full eight hours of sleep. Every baby is going to get through their nights at a different pace. Most pediatricians will recommend that the baby has their own bed in your room for the first six to twelve months to best prevent sudden infant death syndrome, or SIDS. This bed should be free of bumpers, bedding beyond the mattress cover, pillows, and large blankets and stuffed animals.

If Mom is breastfeeding, a show of solidarity can go a long way in keeping your relationship strong; you getting up to do diaper changes while she gets ready to breastfeed will give her that emotional support, and show baby that Mom isn't the only parent that they have to rely on. If Mom has started pumping, or if you've chosen to formula feed, you and Mom can also alternate nights, whether it's switching each night, or being on a

2-2-3 schedule so you can both alternate sleeping in on weekends. It's important—both for your bond with the baby, as well as for the bond with your partner—that they feel they can rely on you.

Bathing

Unlike adults, babies don't tend to need frequent baths. Every family will be different based on their climate, but in colder climates, baby will only need baths if they've gotten fairly messy with spitting up. If you do choose to do daily baths, minimize soaps that can dry out skin, and give them a good amount of baby lotion.

SUPPORTING MOM'S RECOVERY

While the baby is absolutely going to take up a large portion of your time, your partner is going to need every ounce of support, encouragement, and validation that you can muster. Consider that she has just gone through a major medical event that took 40 weeks of anticipation and discomfort to get to; this is then followed by pushing out seven pounds of baby from a very sensitive area. For the next six weeks, the tissues of her cervix, uterus, and vagina are going to be healing, so it is incredibly important to understand that vaginal sex is off the table. When she goes to her six-week postpartum checkup, the doctor will let her know if the healing is sufficient to engage in sex again (yes, even if she had a cesarean), but bear in mind that the cocktail of hormones might mean even if she *can* have sex, she may not be mentally ready. The body continues to reset itself over the next year as the uterus shrinks and organs get back into position, and the hormones alone can make it difficult to get into "the mood."

After a Vaginal Delivery

Two of the hardest things after a vaginal birth are going to the bathroom, and moving around. The first bowel movement is an absolute horror show, especially if Mom had an episiotomy. If you want to help her, make sure there is always a squeeze bottle of warm water accessible to her so that she can reduce the burning of urine in the broken skin if there was tearing. A sitz bath, which is a small tub that is placed over the toilet seat to be filled with warm water—and often baking soda or salt—is going to make it slightly easier. The first bowel movement is extremely painful for most women after a vaginal birth, thanks to the swelling and sensitivity of the tissues, and the soreness of the muscles from doing all the pushing, combined with any stitches and tearing. Stool softeners are likely to be helpful, but it's going to be painful for at the least the first few bowel movements.

Getting up and sitting down can also be an issue while there are sensitive tissues inflamed and sore. Getting a doughnut pillow to sit on can help, and gives Mom a little boost so she doesn't have so far to go when standing and sitting. For a few weeks, Mom might need a bit of help getting up and down from her seat, and may struggle with getting in and out of the car, since it typically means sitting even lower than you would on the couch (with the exception of lifted vehicles, which present their own sitting and stretching issues).

After a C-Section

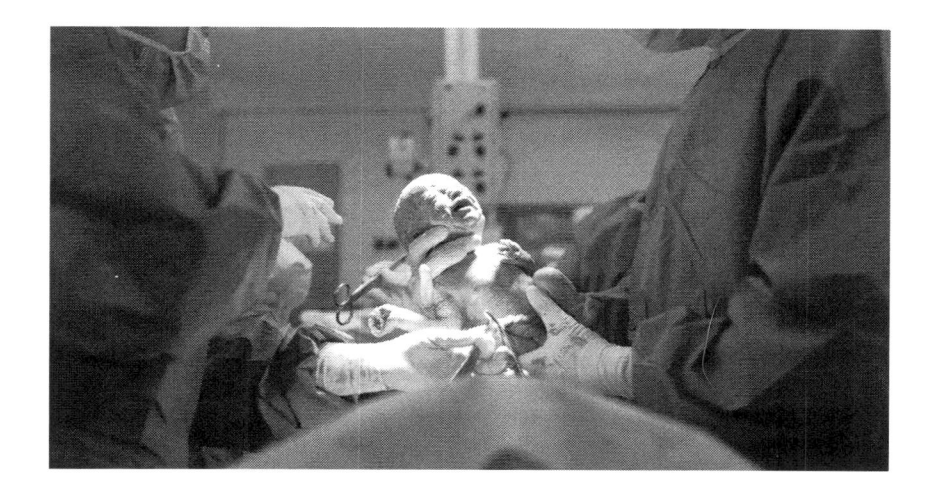

A cesarean is a major abdominal surgery, meaning it's going to take her some time to heal and recover. For the first few weeks, bending down, lifting things heavier than the baby, and general mobility might be difficult for her, so maybe don't ask Mom to bring in the groceries unless it's the bread bag. The body completes its healing from the outside in, so the incision will be healed together long before the incision sites on the organs are completely healed. Even after a cesarean, the body is going to have to reset itself over the next year.

GOING BACK TO WORK

For many couples, Dad goes back to work pretty soon after the baby's arrival, sometimes days to barely weeks after the baby is born. Depending on where you are and what she does for work, Mom might have six weeks to a year on maternity leave. Going back to work is no easy feat for either parent, after having just welcomed a new child into the world. You worry about the bond you have with your baby suffering while you're gone, and missing the big moments, like your baby's first words or steps. There are a thousand things that will race through your head, like missing your baby while you're at work, and worrying about whether or not your partner is holding up okay while you're out of the house.

Keeping Your Bond Strong With Your Baby

After a long day of work, it'd be great to sit back and relax without having to think for a while. Free time is rarely a concept a parent has, and at the baby's young age, bonding is a huge deal. When the baby is a newborn, just getting some snuggle time in and playing tiny sensory games can be great for bonding, as well as letting Mom rest if she's been staying home with the baby. Skin-to-skin contact, baths, and feeding times are great for bonding, and will create memories that you'll grow to cherish as the baby leaves the infant and toddler stages in order to become a whole person on their own.

Consider Her Perspective; Keep Responsibilities Even

Don't be that guy who equates 'mother' to 'maid'. Too many guys say "She's at home with the baby all day while I'm out here working; there's no reason she shouldn't be the one handling the cooking and cleaning," or "I'll just do the nighttime wake ups if I'm off the next day so you can sleep in; I need my sleep so I can go to work." You made this baby together—she just did the hard physical labor of forming and birthing your child, and *you are a team*. Yes, you're going to be tired at work, but so is she. It's better to work together and keep a few more ounces of love and sanity than to flush it down the toilet along with your bond and attachment to your partner.

The argument made at these points, especially when the sleep deprivation and frustration sets in, is usually that all she has to do all day is sit around with the baby. This barely scratches the surface of a stay-at-home parent, especially if they're working from home. If she wants to do anything, whether it's work, taking care of herself, or taking care of the home, it's guaranteed she's going to have to do it while carrying the baby, or be interrupted every five minutes to care for the baby's needs. While you're at work, you can focus your time and energy on the work at hand, while also getting breaks where you can eat your own food on your own. You can go to the bathroom without a baby staring you down. You get your commute where you can enjoy silence or your favorite music without interruption. She gets none of that. Parenting is a full-time job that doesn't stop for either of you, and usually comes with none of the healthcare benefits or paychecks.

When you get home, yes, she's going to want to pass the baby to you so she can go enjoy a shower, put on a show, or have time where she gets to take a break and care for herself. It's easy to dismiss that you're out working for bills to be paid, but she deserves credit for the days where she barely gets a moment to feed herself, for the days where she feels she might break down because the baby just won't sleep, and for the work she's putting in to nurture, raise, and care for her baby and the home. Despite how tired you may be when you get home from work, you also have a child that needs time to bond with you, and who needs your care and attention. You may want nothing more than to sit on the couch with your feet up for an hour, but your child does need you, and your partner needs you to step forward for her and your family. Doing things like taking care of bath time and bedtime so that Mom can finally take a moment to rest is being a good partner and parent. Tackling leftover chores together is a great way to make the home feel like it's not falling apart around your ears, and make your partner feel seen and cared for. Alternating nights with the baby not only allows Mom to catch up on desperately-needed sleep, but gives the baby the security of knowing that when they cry, they have two people they can rely on to hold them, not just one.

CHAPTER 10
NEW DAD HACKS

> "People who say they sleep like a baby usually don't have one." — Leo J. Burke

PREGNANCY HACKS

1. **Schedule ahead**. Feel free to schedule all the needed doctor appointments now. That way it's out of the way and you have a clear schedule and plan for the coming nine months.
2. **Every day 'emergency' bag.** Be ready for day to day morning sickness or indigestion while on the go. Fill a small bag, or toiletry bag with things like snacks, ginger candies, peppermint/lavender essential oils, antacid chews. Keep the bag in the car.
3. **Strengthen your bond before the baby arrives**. There will be less time when the baby is born for you and your spouse. The baby will demand most of the attention. Some ways to strengthen the bond include going on regular dates, learning to deal with conflict, and catering to each other's love language. Strengthening the bond will benefit you and the baby.
4. **Use the experience of other new dads.** Join online or in person new dad groups and learn from other new dads.

NEWBORN HACKS

1. **Bond with baby**. Here are a few bonding activities for dads and newborns. Volunteer for diaper duty and burping duty. Those are excellent bonding times as well as times that mom can get a break. Other ways to bond include skin to skin contact, talking to your baby, and spending as much time with your baby as possible.

2. **Diaper Changing Hack.** One good diaper changing hack is placing a clean diaper underneath the dirty diaper before removing the dirty diaper. That way you can just pull the dirty diaper and clean the baby's bum.
3. **Baby tracker journal or app**. There is a lot to keep track of once baby is born. You need to keep track of feeding, diaper changes, pumping, sleep…
4. **Invest in a good carrier.** A good way to carry baby around and still have our hands free is with a baby carrier. Baby is comforted and we can still get things done… Everyone wins!
5. **Use white noise.** Babies are used to mom's heartbeat, blood whooshing, digestion noises. So a white noise machine provides a familiar environment to fall asleep.
6. **Always have an extra outfit on hand.** Blowouts can happen at any time. Having an extra outfit for those times will be a lifesaver.

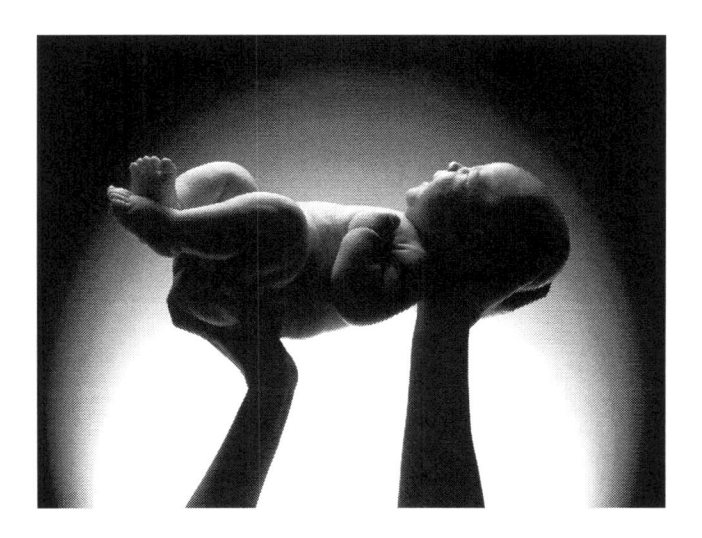

AFTERWORD

Congratulations, Dad! The next 18 years are going to be a rollercoaster, but they're 100% worth it. For right now, you're looking at some of the most amazing moments with Mom and baby. We're talking first words, first steps, trying out new foods, and most importantly, watching your little baby develop into a person. It's an incredible journey, and one of the most fulfilling aspects of life for those who choose to build a family with their partner.

While lots of attention will be focused on the baby, it's important that you take the time for both you, and your relationship with Mom, as the baby grows and you fall into your new routine.

Taking Care of Your Mental Health

Babies are incredibly time consuming. It's important for both you and Mom to be able to take time at least once a week for yourselves; this might mean taking an hour for your hobbies, seeing friends, or finding new ways to meet other parents who understand the journey that you're on. Yes, keeping the house clean is important, but if you're tired, you and Mom can wait to do the dishes or switch the laundry over. Get the rest where you can, even if it's just relaxing in a cuddle puddle on the couch, or curling up in bed for a power nap. Don't fall into believing all the Mommy bloggers who have perfect homes, hair, and makeup who make it seem like the baby has barely changed their lives at all. It's okay to not have it all together, so take the stress off and recognize that as long as the family is cared for, provided for, and has a safe environment, everything is going to be fine. As the baby grows, they'll become more independent, and things like chores will catch up and fall into routine.

Taking Care of Your Relationship

Without the relationship, the family doesn't last. At least, not in the traditional sense. In the first weeks or months, you might not find time to go out for a date night with Mom, but it should definitely be on the agenda. Make plans for when baby is a bit beyond the brand-new baby newborn stage, and keep those on the agenda for when you have someone to watch after the baby that you feel safe with. Be prepared that even if you've just decided to go out for supper, both of you will likely be anxiously checking your phones for any distress calls from whomever is watching over the baby. You may even get an hour in, and both of you may realize you're missing your baby. This is completely normal, and just a part of being a new parent.

Even before you manage to get a date outside of the house, don't let romance die. Stolen kisses and compliments can go a long way. Even if you know you're both going to fall asleep on the couch, doing a movie night together every weekend, or even inviting other couples over for food and board games can keep you feeling connected to each other. Romance is in the little things; love notes written on the mirror, caring for each other by getting the other's favorite snack when you're at the store, or supporting hobbies that you have, especially if you have shared hobbies. Taking a hike, going to the beach, or going out for ice cream as a family is a fantastic way to secure the family bond, and keep the romance alive while you're living life with a new baby.

Most importantly for both your mental health, Mom's mental health, and your relationship is to keep the lines of communication open. You have been Mom's biggest support throughout her pregnancy, and the two of you are a team. Don't let yourself think that signs of sadness or anxiety make you a burden. Talk about your feelings, voice your fears and concerns, and be the same kind of listening board for Mom as well. You've both gone through an incredible change, and it's normal to miss your old life, while simultaneously being in love with your new life. It's an adjustment, so take it easy on yourselves, and seek help when it's needed. You've got this! Welcome to life as a father.

Please leave a review.

If this book has helped you in any way, please leave a review so that others will find the book as well. Thank you for reading.

Scan To Leave Review

Free Bonuses

Free Bonus #1   Baby Financial Planning

In this book, you will learn all about the financial considerations of having a baby.

Free Bonus #2   10 Activities to Learn Parenting Skills

In this book, you will get tips on how to build parenting skills even before the baby is born.

Free Bonus #3 Authentic Connections

In this book, you will learn new skills to help you nurture your connection with your partner and bring it to a whole new level.

To get bonuses, scan this QR code with your cell phone

REFERENCES

What to Expect When You're Expecting, 5th edition, Heidi Murkoff.

American College of Obstetricians and Gynecologists, How to Tell When Labor Begins, May 2020.

National Institutes of Health, Eunice Kennedy Shriver National Institute of Child Health and Human Development, When Does Labor Usually Start?, September 2017.

National Institutes of Health, Eunice Kennedy Shriver National Institute of Child Health and Human Development, About Labor and Delivery, September 2017.

Mayo Clinic, Signs of Labor: Know What to Expect, May 2019.

Mayo Clinic, Stages of Labor and Birth: Baby, It's Time!, February 2020.

Kaiser Permanente, The Four Stages of Labor, January 2019.

REFERENCES

March of Dimes, Stages of Labor, March 2019.

Wiley Online Library, Journal of Midwifery & Women's Health, Ruptured Membranes: When the Bag of Water Breaks, June 2016.

Babylist. (2021, September 22). *Ultimate hospital bag checklist for mom and baby.* https://www.babylist.com/hello-baby/what-to-pack-in-your-hospital-bag

DiProperzio, L., & Srinivasan, H. (2021, September 24). *9 baby items you don't really need to buy.* Parents.

https://www.parents.com/parenting/money/baby-items-you-dont-need/

Ectopic pregnancy - symptoms and causes. (2022, March 12). Mayo Clinic. https://www.mayoclinic.org/diseases-conditions/ectopic-pregnancy/symptoms-causes/syc-20372088#:%7E:text=An%20ectopic%20pregnancy%20occurs%20when,is%20called%20a%20tubal%20pregnancy.

Infertility | reproductive health | CDC. (n.d.). CDC.

https://www.cdc.gov/reproductivehealth/infertility/index.htm#:%7E:text=What%20is%20infertility%3F,6%20months%20of%20unprotected%20sex.

Marple, K. (n.d.). *Pregnancy week by week.* Baby Center.

https://www.babycenter.com/pregnancy/week-by-week

Methods of childbirth. (2004, June 7). WebMD.

https://www.webmd.com/baby/guide/delivery-methods

Mirchandani, A. (2021, October 12). *6 ways dad can prep for pregnancy*. Motherly. https://www.mother.ly/life/dad-prep-for-pregnancy/

Miscarriage - symptoms and causes. (2021, October 16). Mayo Clinic. https://www.mayoclinic.org/diseases-conditions/pregnancy-loss-miscarriage/symptoms-causes/syc-20354298#:%7E:text=About%2010%20to%2020%20percent,even%20know%20about%20a%20pregnancy.

Montgomery, N. (n.d.). *Future fathers: 9 ways to help her get pregnant*. Baby Center. https://www.babycenter.com/getting-pregnant/preparing-for-pregnancy/future-fathers-9-ways-to-help-her-get-pregnant_1347929

Pregnancy week-by-week. (n.d.). The Bump.

https://www.thebump.com/pregnancy-week-by-week

Reporter, G. S. (2020, June 30). *I started the "gender reveal party" trend. And i regret it*. The Guardian.

https://www.theguardian.com/lifeandstyle/2020/jun/29/jenna-karvunidis-i-started-gender-reveal-party-trend-regret

What are some common complications of pregnancy? (2021, April 20). National Institute of Child Health and Human Development.

https://www.nichd.nih.gov/health/topics/pregnancy/conditioninfo/complications

What health problems can develop during pregnancy? (2017, January 31). National Institute of Child Health and Human Development.

https://www.nichd.nih.gov/health/topics/preconceptioncare/conditioninfo/health-problems

What to Expect. (n.d.). *Screenings and tests during pregnancy.*

https://www.whattoexpect.com/pregnancy/screenings-and-tests-during-pregnancy/

Brumbaugh DE, Arruda J, Robbins K, Ir D, Santorico SA, Robertson CE, Frank DN. "Mode of Delivery Determines Neonatal Pharyngeal Bacterial Composition and Early Intestinal Colonization." *J Pediatr Gastroenterol Nutr* 2016 Mar 28. [Epub ahead of print] PubMed PMID: 27035381.

Switzerland. World Health Organization. "WHO statement on cesarean section rates." Apr. 2015. http://www.who.int/reproductivehealth/publications/maternal_perinatal_health/cs-statement/en/.

United States. Centers for Disease Control and Prevention. "Pregnancy-Related Deaths." Jan. 12, 2016. http://www.cdc.gov/reproductivehealth/maternalinfanthealth/pregnancy-relatedmortality.htm.

Test Tube Image

United States. U.S. Department of Health and Human Services. Centers for Disease Control and Prevention. Hamilton, B.H., et al. "Births: Final Data for 2014." Dec. 12, 2015. http://www.cdc.gov/nchs/data/nvsr/nvsr64/nvsr64_12.pdf.

ABOUT THE AUTHOR

New Dad Support consists of dads and parenting professionals and experts whose passion is sharing their experience and expertise with new dads and dads-to-be.

Made in the USA
Monee, IL
12 August 2024

5a31262f-90e4-40e5-9c3f-4b343a3011bcR01